M000315099

A guide to recent architecture

• • •

Suzanne Strum
Photographs by Diego Ferrari

Barcelona

A guide to recent architecture

• • • **ellipsis**

•••

All rights reserved. No part of this publication may be reproduced in any form without written permission from the publisher

BRITISH LIBRARY CATALOGUING IN PUBLICATION
A CIP record for this book is available from the British Library

PUBLISHED BY •••ellipsis
2 Rufus Street London N1 6PE
E MAIL ...@ellipsis.co.uk
www http://www.ellipsis.com
SERIES EDITOR Tom Neville
SERIES DESIGN Jonathan Moberly
EDITOR Rosa Ainley

COPYRIGHT © 2001 Ellipsis London Limited

PRINTING AND BINDING Hong Kong

ISBN 1 84166 005 1

•••ellipsis is a trademark of Ellipsis
London Limited

For a copy of the Ellipsis catalogue or
information on special quantity orders
of Ellipsis books please contact
sales on 020 7739 3157 or sales@ellipsis.co.uk

Suzanne Strum 2001

Contents

Introduction

The projects in this guide demonstrate the ambitious cultural and urban programmes carried out in Barcelona since the death of Franco in 1975. Nearly 40 years of dictatorship and isolation ended with the restoration of democracy, propelling whirlwind changes and the push to modernisation that marked the Spanish transition. During this time the country looked beyond its own borders, entering NATO and the European Community. By the mid 1980s, the economy was on a dramatic upswing.

Internally, the transition led to the resurgence of regional identities. The regional autonomy granted in 1980 – covering domestic trade and economics, planning, housing, public works, transport systems, public space, and regional development – was a decisive factor for transformation in Barcelona, the capital of Spain's north-eastern region of Catalunya. After years of repression Catalan language and culture were revitalised. Barcelona's first democratic city elections since the civil war took place in 1979 and the public sector became the guiding force in creating new identity and recovering lost traditions. Mayor Narcis Serra and his successor Pascal Maragall formed a critical alliance with architects. Viewing contemporary Europe as made up of constellations of cities in competition with each other, they recognised the urban realm as an essential field of actuation. Jordi Pujol's conservative nationalist party controlling the regional government, the Generalitat, was set in tense competition with a socialist city hall – a situation that still exists today.

In the 1980s, for the first time, Catalan design became a significant presence on the international scene, providing an alternative to the predominant strains of post-modernism. New-found prosperity fuelled a local design boom in fashion, interiors and furniture; the construction of networks of public architecture and urban foci generated much interest. After decades of neglect in the public sector, architects developed proposals for the enrichment of the city's urban realm in collaboration with other professionals. The first of three phases of urban renewal projects was launched.

Urban policy placed an emphasis on the creation of public space in response to Barcelona's urban history, morphology and growth. The strategy in this first phase was to consider the city as already constructed but to tackle the problem of urban chaos by considering the existing urban imprint and layers, and to deal with the lack of planning criteria, a legacy of the Franco years. Due to its geographical limits, bounded to the south and north by the Llobregat and Besòs rivers, to the west and east by the Collserola mountain range and Mediterranean sea, Barcelona is a city of high density.

The first phase of renewal was orchestrated by the architect Oriol Bohigas, head of urban planning in the first democratic city administration. He created new urban strategies based on a detailed analysis of the city's past forms and neighbourhoods, and these also came to characterise the later phases of renewal as well. Barcelona's distinct urban form had in fact originated some 2000 years earlier in a compact Roman *oppidum*. The walled medieval centre grew up from there with an economy strongly linked to maritime activities. By the mid nineteenth century, growth spawned by industrialisation necessitated the demolition of the walls and the city's expansion, which was begun in 1859.

Following an abstract gridded plan by the engineer and urban theorist Ildefons Cerdá, the 'Eixample' (Catalan for expansion) was composed of 550 square blocks and major arteries that increased the city to ten times its original size, filling out the alluvial plane between sea and mountain and incorporating outlying independent towns. The most central part, straddling Passeig de Gracia, became the context in which modernist

Barcelona: a guide to recent architecture

masters Lluís Domènech i Montaner and Antoni Gaudí built the ostentatious homes for the turn-of-the-century nouveaux riches.

The urbanisation of two large districts of the city was carried out when Barcelona hosted the World Expositions of 1888 and 1929. The 1888 fair transformed the Ciutadella, the military fort bordering the old city to the north, into parkland. A breeding ground for modernism, the Exposition brought change to a whole city sector between two symbolic points – the Arc de Triomf monumental gateway and the Columbus Statue, the waterfront terminus of the historic centre's main thoroughfare, the Ramblas. For the 1929 Exposition the mountain of Montjuic was tamed into one of gardened urbanity.

In 1936 the civil war interrupted progressive planning initiatives in the city and by 1939 the triumphant Franco changed the names of streets, removing and destroying symbolic and commemorative sculptures. From the 1950s on industrialisation once again led to rampant urban growth. Driven by private speculation, the city edges were built up, yet were unplanned. These areas were the first to be addressed in the regeneration programme.

The projects outlined by Bohigas were a reaction to the Franco years. Mass immigration to industrialising Barcelona from other areas of Spain had resulted in urban chaos: low-cost housing built by developers, shanty towns and slab blocks sprung up without the benefits of urban connection or amenities. These marginalised zones became the sites for the 'Projects without Plans'. Proceeding neighbourhood by neighbourhood, these were low-cost, small-scale, short-term interventions aiming to 'monumentalise' the outlying areas of the city. In each barrio traditional symbolic references were restored and new ones created. These were finishing touches rather than broad strokes; public art by local and international artists in collaboration with the team of young municipal architects enhanced the projects.

A second phase of regeneration which carried on and enlarged this strategy began with Barcelona's selection in 1986 to host the 1992 Olympics. This jump-started the large-scale transformations prefigured in the city's 1976 Metropolitan Plan. Drawn up in the period of late Francismo, the plan reserved open spaces and delineated the large tracts of land acquired by the public administration. Such foresight allowed for full-scale modernisation and upgrading. Twelve 'new centres' were outlined from the spaces at the edge of the city and included the four Olympic sport zones: Montjuic, Diagonal, Vall d'Hebron, and the Olympic Port and Village. The city was opened up towards the sea: the waterfront was transformed into a continuous promenade of more than 4 kilometres for recreation and dwelling. This coincided with projects aiming to create new cultural institutions, reusing and renovating existing buildings and constructing others to house them. Long plagued by social problems and decay, the Ciutat Vella was regenerated as the city's symbolic centre. In the Eixample area, which is only being finished now with the extension of the Diagonal to the sea, gaps needed to be filled and extensions made.

The Olympic period was consciously modelled on the tradition of making use of ephemeral events to experiment with new urbanism, as had occurred in the World Expositions of 1888 and 1929. The ability of the projects to influence their surroundings and act as catalysts to further change was a priority. Attention to detail meant that work proceeded on all scales: from urban furnishings and paving, kiosks and sculptures to metropolitan intercommunications. Projects were awarded through competitions to a generation that had cut their professional teeth on

Barcelona: a guide to recent architecture

private homes, mixed with figures of international renown following the postmodern prescription of the time.

In a broader Spanish context, 1992 saw the culmination of the post-Franco transition with a volley of high-profile events: the 500th anniversary of the discovery of the Americas, the Barcelona Olympics, the Seville Expo, Madrid as Europe's Cultural Capital, and the diffusion and promotion of Spanish culture abroad including architecture, film, fashion, art and design – even a Catalan 'top model'.

Emergent political, economic and institutional structures coincided with architectural projects in Olympic Barcelona. The city government oversaw the expansion of the public realm, thus going against the current of privatisation prevalent elsewhere. Based on decentralisation and difference and set within a social context of active neighbourhood associations, volunteer culture and civic participation, the massive reconstruction was largely uncontentious. With the restoration of local traditions and festivals and the invention of new ones such as the *corre foc*, a Catalan version of Pamplona's running of the bulls featuring devils, dragons and fireworks, public space became once again a place of congregation.

The projects of the Olympic period also sought to rekindle the city's connection with the modern movement with the reconstruction of Mies van der Rohe's 1929 Pavilion (see page 5.6) and Josep Lluís Sert and Lluís Lacasa's Pavilion of the Second Republic (see page 10.28). Sert was the major force behind the GATPAC, a group of young architects who promoted the avant-garde within the progressive context of the Republic in the early 1930s, whose activities were cut short by the civil war. After studying with Le Corbusier in Paris, Sert brought his mentor to Barcelona to create the Plan Macia. Proposing a restructuring of the city based on zoning, the plan introduced a new superblock modelled on the Ville Radieuse.

To understand some of the characteristics of contemporary architecture in Barcelona, beyond the political and urban armature, some highwater marks and influential figures should be mentioned from the otherwise architecturally stagnant Franco years. Excluded from the post-war reconstruction taking place in the rest of Europe, the activities of Grup R initiated in 1951 were an early sign of renewal after the civil war. José Antonio Coderch, Oriol Bohigas, Joaquim Gili and Antoni Moragas, among others, identified with Italian Realism, situating architecture in an expanded cultural critique, and opening up a spirit of debate that would later be essential during the transition to democracy. A respected teacher, Coderch became an influential figure on the architectural scene, infusing modern language with the organic vernacular. A controversial figure due to his sympathies with the regime, this also permitted him international ties as a member of CIAM and Team X. Bohigas emerged as one of the leading intellectuals of Barcelona's reconstruction, one of a group of multidisciplinary activists who formulated a vision of the city against a backdrop of autocracy. An architect, planner, and combative cultural critic, he influenced a generation. More recently, Rafael Moneo might be added to these as recipient of the 1996 Pritzker Prize (the architectural world's equivalent of the Nobel Prize), as Spain's most important international architect, and for his teaching at the architecture school during the 1970s on context, typology, individuality and detail.

Barcelona's panorama of contemporary architecture is an evolving response to all these influences. In the early stages, Kenneth Frampton placed Catalan architecture under the rubric of 'critical regionalism' for its tectonics, 'laconic lines' and sensitive response to setting. Others emphasised its cosmopolitan civility and viewed the projects as a blend of restrained minimalism, rationalism and eclectic contextualism. Critics

Barcelona: a guide to recent architecture

saw Spain as an architect's paradise, attributing the high level of design to the respect and control that Spanish practitioners exercised under professional and legal structures that are only now being liberalised. Catalan architecture is marked by an underlying concern for technical issues, problem solving and an economy of forms and systems. But its most singular characteristics in the best projects of recent years are topographical: the incorporation and extension of a building into its site to form a new landscape and an approach to the design of infrastructure that sees it as a hybrid of engineering, architecture and land art.

Many of the architects in this guide are professors at ETSAB, the Universitat Politecnica de Catalunya's architecture school; they are also engaged in multiple activities: practice, historical research, criticism, publishing, exhibitions. Many have become important international figures: Ignasi de Solà-Morales was instrumental in creating a framework of theoretical interchange and the late Enric Miralles with Benedetta Tagliabue has won major commissions abroad. With its broad European outlook, *Quaderns*, the journal of the architects' association, played an important role in stimulating debate and disseminating ideas under the direction of Josep Lluís Mateo during the Olympic period and Manuel Gausa in the 1990s.

The post-Olympic period has been marked by polarisation rather than consensus. Following in the wake of 1992 was the third phase of urban strategies: the mega-scale strategic development projects under way now. These are set against immense housing developments, high rises, shopping centres, multi-use containers, theme parks, and commercial zones driven by private investment – seen as a threat to architectural quality.

With a jump in scale, the redefinition of the city within its territory involves the redevelopment of the riverside with a stress on sustainability. The Besòs connection with the sea awaits completion by the facilities for the so-called 'Forum of Cultures 2004' which is following the already exhausted notion that an ephemeral 'event' must once again stimulate urban development. The altered course of the Llobregat river will permit the enlargement of the industrial port and airport, and the arrival of the high-speed train will transform the Sagrera area into an international and regional transport node. Most of these operations fall under the direction of the present head of municipal urbanism Josep Antonio Acebillo, who began his career as one of the 'golden pencils', the talented crop of graduates who formed Bohigas' first municipal team.

But many have questioned Barcelona's far-flung success that has more than doubled tourism, attracted trade shows and congresses, overburdening existing infrastructure and causing the theme-parking of the centre. Overscaled interventions and the massive demolition of labyrinthine quarters lead important writers to decry the loss of the city's unique patina. Although a strong cultural filter has always been applied to any foreign models being imposed, its effects now appear to be weakening, resulting in homogenisation. Regional Barcelona is composed of a dizzying number of municipalities, making development control virtually impossible at a metropolitan level. New resettlement patterns reflect the exorbitant increase in real-estate values: the city is losing its youthful population to the suburbs while the centre has become home to new populations from Africa, China, and Pakistan. Barcelona, which always considered itself a 'peripheral city' in the most positive sense is succumbing to the same pressures that occur everywhere else.

For building the future on to the past the city has won important accolades normally reserved for individuals – Harvard University's Prince Charles Award in 1993 and the RIBA gold medal in 1999. Barcelona's reconstruction was based on the primacy of the city as the significant cultural

Barcelona: a guide to recent architecture

and political agent in a globalised age and its success has served as a model for the regeneration of other Spanish cities such as Bilbao and Valencia.

As for the younger generation of architects, they operate in a wholly new globalised and digitalised context. Recently the alarm was sounded in the press that while Madrid was passing the 'relevo' (the baton) on to the next generation, Barcelona was folding in on itself. On a political level as well, the waning force of the regional mandate seems to be reinforcing Madrid's centralism under the right-wing Partido Popular. But recent indications suggest that some of the architects on the cusp of 40 will participate with invited international 'stars' in building the 'Forum of Cultures 2004' and the city will address these new challenges with renewed vitality and debate.

ACKNOWLEDGEMENTS
My thanks to Xavier Costa for involving me in this project and also to all of the architects that I contacted with my questions.

Barcelona: a guide to recent architecture

Using this book

This guide is divided into 13 sections, which are based on neighbourhoods but also follow the flow of projects of the last few years and so may overlap from one district to another. The first 11 are areas within the city limits. Sections 11 and 12 are within the broader metropolitan area but still linked to the city by public transport. Section 13 is an hour's excursion away by car or by train to the Catalan town of Igualada.

The first sections overlap with the traditional itinerary of the Barcelona visitor, while some later entries will take you to the city's borders – many recent projects are concentrated in these neighbourhoods which fall far outside the normal tourist routes. Most maps do not include such a broad view of the city so I recommend buying the *Barcelona Official Map* from Turisme de Barcelona, the only plan which goes as far as the ring roads or Rondas. It also has the advantage of marking the location of many of the projects included here. You can buy it in one of the three tourist information offices: Plaça Catalunya, 17-s (open 9.00–21.00); Plaça Sant Jaume, Ciutat 2 (open Monday to Saturday, 10.00–20.00; Sunday, 10.00–14.00); Sants Railway Station (open Monday to Friday, 8.00–20.00; Saturday and Sunday, 8.00–14.00).

In most areas, projects are grouped together and are within walking distance of each other. Both metro and bus lines are given. You can buy multi-trip tickets for public transport and maps of the system in tobacconists' shops and metro stations. A T10 ten-trip card for bus and metro is half the cost of paying for individual trips. The Barcelona Bus Turístic offers two linked routes with stops at the city's most important sites of interest. A one- or two-day pass offers unlimited travel: you may get on and off as you wish, however the route does not reach many of the entries within this book.

Renting a bicycle in the Ribera neighbourhood and follow the indicated cycle routes is a pleasant and practical way to tour the projects along the city's 4-kilometre waterfront.

Finally, useful websites to consult when planning a trip are: www.barcelonaturisme.com and www.bcn.es. The latter is the city's own site where you can zoom into detailed maps of each sector of the city to find public facilities and institutions.

Ciutat Vella

Museu d'Història de la Ciutat Addition

The museum's entrance is on Plaça del Rei, through the sixteenth-century Casa Padellàs, a merchant's palace that was moved here stone by stone from Mercaders Street. The palace was saved from destruction when Via Laietana was cut through the old city. Above ground, the museum, dedicated to conservation of the city's heritage, is composed of a complex of medieval structures enclosing the plaza, including a romanesque tower, the gothic Saló Tinell civil throne room, and the Santa Àgata chapel.

The extensive subterranean level reveals archaeological vestiges and imprints from the Roman to the paleo-Christian period. Llínas' intervention, which was awarded the Barcelona City Prize in 1998, added 2000 square metres to the museum's underground space, highlighting the layers and superimpositions of Barcelona's 2000-year history, starting from the remains of the walled oppidum of Colonia Iulia Augusta Faventia Paterna Barcino.

Llínas expanded a route under the Carrer Comptes, the Plaça Sant Iu, the Mares Museum and part of the cathedral, where some of the most important paleo-Christian remains in Europe were discovered. The architect's goal was to make the walls and ceiling surrounding these important finds 'disappear'. The visitor passes through the neutralised container on metal walkways and bridges. These overlook each element of the archaeological complex, now highlighted.

ADDRESS Plaça del Rei
METRO L4 Jaume I
BUS 16, 17, 19, 40, 45
ACCESS open October to June: Tuesday to Saturday, 10.00–14.00 and 16.00–20.00; July to September: Tuesday to Saturday, 10.00–20.00; Sunday, 10.00–14.00

Josep Llínas 1994–95

Ciutat Vella

Josep Llínas 1994–95

Centre Cìvic Pati Llimona

The restoration and transformation into civic centres of two nobles' palaces on different streets involved a series of microsurgical operations along the Roman wall. These laid bare layers of the city's past. The rehabilitation opposed the monumental criteria employed at the turn of the century when the Via Laietana was cut through the gothic quarter, privileging Roman remains at the cost of the adjacent medieval structures and later buildings. These procedures had resulted in the destruction of medieval fabric as the Roman wall was isolated as a monument and surrounded by a tree-lined promenade.

This operation offered different criteria. It was conceived as an archaeological narrative: opening up two plazas, inside and outside of the Roman city walls, as well as a section of medieval street that had been bricked up since the eighteenth century. The arch of the Roman pedestrian entry gate leading from the sea to Barcino's Decumanus is now visible. The Roman wall with two towers and the original gates with medieval and renaissance windows were restored. Layers of time have been peeled back: Roman remains are displayed from Regomir Street by a glass floor and window revealing the internal façade of a third tower adjacent to the gate and the semi-circular base of the first tower dating back to the reign of Augustus.

Visitors enter the first noble's residence from Carrer del Regomir through a small passage leading to a courtyard. It dates back to the twelfth century and was the residence of the Marc family, who controlled the gold trade in Barcelona. At the end of the thirteenth century it became the property of the Gualbes, a merchant family who held important city posts until the eighteenth century. Marc family emblems still adorn the second-floor rooms and arched ground floor. One wing of the palace was demolished in the nineteenth century when a major extension was built. The resto-

Ignasi de Solà-Morales 1987–91

Ignasi de Solà-Morales 1987–91

Centre Cívic Pati Llimona

ration involved eliminating divisions and additions to recover the essential spaces, especially two large medieval halls on the second floor. A stair and elevator were added for public use. A ramp leads visitors down to the Roman remains covered by glass on the street. These new elements were conceived as superimpositions on to the old.

The second, sixteenth-century palace is entered from the Correu Vell street. It belonged to the Ferran family who were put in charge of the city's postal service by Emperor Charles v. The typical courtyard building has been restored to its original structure after having been converted into an apartment building. The main façade with wrought-iron balconies has rococo graffito decoration from the end of the eighteenth century.

The most spectacular space is the second plaza entered from a narrow street bordering the civic centre. The space is dramatically enclosed by the perimeter of the Roman wall.

ADDRESS Carrer del Regomir, 3/Carrer Sant Simplici/Carrer Correu Vell, 5
METRO L4 Jaume I
BUS 17, 40, 45
ACCESS open

Ignasi de Solà-Morales 1987–91

Ignasi de Solà-Morales 1987–91

Museu d'Art Contemporani de Barcelona (MACBA)

The creation of the MACBA was a key piece in the regeneration of the Raval area, traditionally inhabited by immigrant groups and industrial workshops. The creation of this new contemporary art museum brings to mind the gentrification of Les Halles in Paris with the Pompidou Centre and the resulting tensions between an elite institution and the mix of neighbourhood people who occupy the plaza when school finishes.

The museum forms part of a cultural axis of new institutions meant to draw people into the area and which have radically transformed it. Public money poured in and expropriations were carried out over a long period, opening up gaps in the high-density fabric. Now, with investment from the private sector, galleries, restaurants and boutiques have clustered around the institutional axis which leads from the Liceu Opera House, past the medieval courtyard of the former hospital of Santa Creu (now housing the National Library and the Massana art school), the Convent dels Àngels and the Centre de Cultural Contemporània, to new university buildings before ending in the Plaça de la Universitat.

The museum was founded by a consortium including the Barcelona City Hall, the Generalitat and the MACBA Foundation. Highly visible projects were commissioned from internationally known architects during the Olympic period, and here the city selected Richard Meier, originally one of the New York Five, who in the 1970s explored the formal revision of Le Corbusier's early purist architecture with a focus on transparency. Meier is the author of many cultural buildings in the US and Europe, including the Frankfurt Design Museum and the Getty Center in Los Angeles.

MACBA faces an enormous plaza that was opened up between the site of the Convent dels Àngels and the Casa de Caritat (see page 1.12).

Richard Meier & Partners 1987–95

Museu d'Art Contemporani de Barcelona (MACBA)

Richard Meier & Partners 1987–95

Museu d'Art Contemporani de Barcelona (MACBA)

Against its urban backdrop, Meier's signature building is an elegant and pristine white sculptural work that stands out from everything around it. The building gestures to the public space with transparent layers: a glazed façade, and a monumental ramp to all levels behind set within an immense longitudinal atrium. In addition to the three double-height exhibition floors the museum also has a basement level with an auditorium. Seven floors of offices and services occupy a block to the left of the entry where mezzanine levels were added.

The building's mass has been cut into and sculpted, playing off of interior and exterior space. A circular entry hall faces the interior garden. Various sculptural forms puncture the screen wall of the main façade with a balcony terrace over the entrance, the glass curtain wall, and an organic shaped exhibition hall. More discreet exhibition spaces and elegant circular forms are set beyond the main atrium. Unfortunately, given the Mediterranean light levels many windows have been blinded and interventions into the columned interior have been made to accommodate exhibitions and to be able to hang art works. The third-floor skylights have been painted black.

ADDRESS Plaça dels Àngels, 1
METRO L1, L2, L3, FFCC, Catalunya
BUS 14, 16, 38, 59
ACCESS open Monday, Wednesday, Thursday and Friday, 11.00–19.30; Saturday, 10.00–20.00; Sunday, 10.00–15.00; closed on Tuesday

Richard Meier & Partners 1987–95

Ciutat Vella

Richard Meier & Partners 1987–95

Centre de Cultura Contemporània (CCCB)

The Olympic period did not only involve outer neighbourhoods. It also opened up and regenerated the historic centre. Lluís Clotet and Òscar Tusquets' 1980 plan, 'From the Liceu to the Seminar', proposed the creation of new cultural institutions within historic buildings. On this side of the Ramblas many abandoned religious structures have been so reused.

The CCCB, inaugurated in 1994, is set in an old orphanage, part of a complex known as the Casa de Caritat (House of Charity). It offers exhibitions on everything from Joyce's Dublin to new cultures of work, and sponsors film, dance and music festivals, lectures and walking tours.

The architects inserted a dramatic glass volume to finish the courtyard building, which dates back to 1804. Entered through the Pati de les Dones or Woman's Patio, three wings of the historic building have been restored to house offices, seminar rooms and exhibition spaces. The new north wing has a horizontally gridded glass façade with a tilted cornice that breaks the sense of enclosure with reflected views of city and sea. Lifts and escalators with outside views occupy the new wing. Above is the Sala Mirador, a reception room offering panoramic views of Ciutat Vella.

The unusual entrance to the exhibition spaces leads from the courtyard, treated as a diptych with two colours of paving stone and a bench, to a concrete ramp. Multimedia screenings are shown in an enormous concrete reception area underground. The courtyard leads to a public back garden bordered by the MACBA (see page 1.8) and a private university building. The centre has an excellent website: www.cccb.org.

ADDRESS Carrer Montalegre, 3–5
METRO L1, L2, L3, FFCC, Catalunya BUS 9, 14, 18, 38, 47, 58, 59, 91
ACCESS open Tuesday, Thursday, Friday, 11.00–14.00, 16.00–20.00;
Wednesday and Saturday, 11.00–20.00; Sunday, 11.00–19.00

Viaplana and Piñón 1990–93

Ciutat Vella

Viaplana and Piñón 1990–93

FAD

Lluís Clotet began working on the renovation of the medieval Convent dels Àngels back in 1982, but it wasn't until the FAD (El Foment de les Artes Decoratives) took it over in 1999 that it had a tenant and clear use. The building was restored and added to, following the guidelines proposed by Clotet and Tusquets in their study on the reuse of existing historic buildings in the Raval. Then public administration changes interrupted the project and left it vacant for years. The convent's lateral façade and the small additions form the backdrop to the Plaça dels Àngels and Richard Meier's white purist-object building, the MACBA (see page 1.8). The volumes, annexes and façade treatments form a pastiche that recalls the accretion of buildings over time that created such historic spaces as the Plaça del Rei.

In the project's last phase, the architects renovated the interior to serve as headquarters for the FAD organisation founded in Barcelona in 1903, dedicated to the promotion of design. The FAD awards prestigious yearly prizes in architecture and graphics and, with this central location, now assumes a more public profile. Exhibitions are displayed in the restored ground-floor hall and lectures are held in the upper-level multipurpose room with offices in between. The building and decorative materials for this project were donated by the manufacturers. The annex perpendicular to the convent will become a library for the Diputació of Barcelona and the chapel is shared by different public institutions for special events.

ADDRESS Plaça dels Àngels
METRO L1, L2, L3, FFCC, Catalunya
BUS 9, 14, 18, 38, 47, 58, 59, 91
ACCESS open

Lluís Clotet and Ignacio Paricio 1982–99

Lluís Clotet and Ignacio Paricio 1982–99

Blanquerna Faculty of Communication Sciences

The Blanquerna school building has a chameleon-like quality. The adjustable aluminum façade of the school changes with the needs of its users. The aluminum panels set in front of the windows may be mechanically opened to 85 degrees, lowered or completely shut according to the requirements of the lecture rooms within. When closed, the panels form a continuous skin; when open they create a random composition of horizontal bandings.

This classroom building for the private Ramon Llull University makes good use of the newly created public garden that it borders and encloses along with the MACBA, the CCCB and the Antic Theatre (see pages 1.8 and 1.12). The glazed ground-floor bar decorated in warm orange and yellow tones connects visually with the garden's grid of trees and banded earthen ground. A stair on this façade leads to basement media production studios including image and sound production, control rooms, a photographic laboratory and seven video-editing rooms.

The building envelope was determined by a masterplan and is formed by a long building set parallel to Joaquim Costa Street against a retaining wall that has been left bare in the garden, used to rectify the change in levels between the site and the street behind. Its longitudinal elevation faces the garden façade of the Casa de Caritat and overhangs the ground-floor level.

The faculty has been designed as a sleek aluminum bar, separated from the adjacent buildings and retaining wall through the use of gaps, treated as intermediate volumes of glass. One of the glass volumes stretches slightly out to form the main entry off the Carrer Valldonzella. The other glass gap is set next to the wider volume and forms the circulation zones, administration and offices before ending in a sky-lit library on the first

D Freixes, V Miranda, V Bou, E González 1994–96

D Freixes, V Miranda, V Bou, E González 1994–96

floor. Next to this, the main volume houses the ground-floor cafeteria, bar and classrooms. Next to the library on the first floor are large lecture rooms. The second and third floors have classrooms set against a curved wall and seminar rooms occupy the fourth floor.

ADDRESS Carrer Valldonzella, 23
METRO L1, L2, L3, FFCC, Catalunya
BUS 9, 14, 18, 38, 47, 58, 59, 91
ACCESS none

D Freixes, V Miranda, V Bou, E González 1994–96

Ciutat Vella

D Freixes, V Miranda, V Bou, E González 1994–96

Ras Gallery

Ras is a bookstore and gallery dedicated to contemporary architecture, design and photography. It reflects the interests and professional activities of its owners, ACTAR, a publishing company formed by innovative graphic designers and photographers specialising in books with the same themes. Ras is one of many galleries, bookstores, restaurants and design shops located on Doctor Dou and in the surrounding area that have gathered around the new art-related institutions here, making the Raval an art and design centre.

This ground-floor space has cast-iron columns. The design intervention is made with minimal gestures and elements. An entry zone is divided from the back exhibition area by a bookcase of curving steel and polycarbonate panels displaying ACTAR's own books as well as a selection of international publications. A wire-mesh mat stands out against the polished concrete floor.

The exhibition programming is closely related to ACTAR's own book-publishing activities. The informal lectures and presentations made here make Ras one of the few non-institutional forums for architecture in the city.

ADDRESS Carrer del Doctor Dou, 10
METRO L1, L3, FFCC Catalunya
BUS 14, 18, 38, 59
ACCESS Tuesday to Saturday, 11.00–14.00, 16.00–20.00

Jaime Salazar 1998

Jaime Salazar 1998

Social Housing on Carrer del Carme

This project is one of the most interesting examples of new social housing to appear in the Raval neighbourhood, responding to questions of urban and social quality. The architect made the decision not to occupy the maximum building envelope allowed by the municipal code. Instead, he freed up part of the site to improve the character of Carrer d'en Roig, a narrow street flanked by four-, five- and six-storey buildings. This street-level void, carved out of the corner volume at the meeting point of Carrers del Carme and d'en Roig, is his main urban gesture, creating an inviting entrance to the narrow sidestreet.

The apartments could have occupied one continuous volume. Instead a new housing typology has been explored and introduced into the area. The apartments have been broken down into three blocks of varied heights, set back at different levels on Carrer d'en Roig on a one-storey commercial base, creating terraces for the first-floor apartments. A wall of wooden shutters screens open spaces from the street. This new typology brings sunlight into the block and creates communal courtyards.

In the interiors, the living spaces have been set at the corners, with full-length windows giving views to the street. The horizontal banding marking the floor levels, the cream-coloured stucco and the green wooden shutters are traditional elements that blend the moulded volumetric building into its surroundings. The building is close to the newly inaugurated Rambla of the Raval which demolished buildings to open up a wide urban esplanade in the neighbourhood.

ADDRESS Carrer del Carme, 55–57/Carrer d'en Roig, 28–30
METRO L1, L3, FFCC, Catalunya
BUS 14, 18, 38, 59
ACCESS none

Josep Llínas 1993–95

Ciutat Vella

Josep Llínas 1993–95

Gran Teatre del Liceu

On 31 January 1994 a crowd gathered on the Ramblas to watch as this emblematic building went up in smoke – not the first time the opera house had been destroyed by fire. Miguel Garriga i Roca's design, which opened in 1844, contained a horseshoe-shaped Italian auditorium, the second largest in the world after Milan's La Scala. Originally built by a group of military singers, the building burned and was reconstructed in 1861 by Josep Oriol Mestres i Esplugas.

Architect, theorist and historian Ignasi de Solá-Morales had been working for years on a plan for the building's renovation and enlargement when he was awarded the reconstruction project. The Licèu's consortium took the nostalgic decision to create a replica of the hall, while the fire made modernisation possible. Expropriation of buildings on adjoining sites allowed for enlargement especially of the stage, which is now equipped with state-of-the-art technology. Facilities and equipment for recordings and filming were an important part of the updating; the hollow curved concrete theatre wall serves for installations. The replicated hall exists within a new steel structure that dealt with the technical problems caused by building on an aquifer (foundations under groundwater level). Additional circulation elements were added, along with a giant foyer to hold all the spectators during intervals. New façades of cream-coloured stone and green marble wrap the street face, housing the management offices behind, and connect to the preserved entrance hall.

ADDRESS La Rambla, 61–65
METRO L3 Liceu
BUS 14, 38, 59
ACCESS open with admission to opera
WEBSITE www.liceubarcelona.com

Ignasi de Solà-Morales, Lluís Dilmé, Xavier Fabré 1994–99

Ignasi de Solà-Morales, Lluís Dilmé, Xavier Fabré 1994–99

Taxidermista Cafè Restaurant

Located in one of the corners of the Plaça Reial, just off the Ramblas, this café and restaurant is one of a series of new establishments that spill out under the arcades and enliven the public arena. This lively plaza, frequented by a broad social mix, was cut into the fabric of the historic city on the site of an old convent between 1848–59. The lamp posts are by Gaudí – his only public commission. The plaza was repaved in the 1980s by Federico Correa and Alfonso Milá.

The restaurant's name reveals the building's past life. Skeletons were reconstructed in the basement, the taxidermist's workshop was in the apartment above, and the ground-floor store sold educational specimens.

The restaurant was designed by the architect Beth Galí who has carried out such important public commissions as the Joan Miró Park library. The designer has stripped the wooden beams and left the vaulted ceiling. An 'atrium' has been cut into the centre, up to the apartment above, where a stair descends to the basement. The tables surrounding this void are set over glass floors, with a view to the space below. A steel circular stair marks the end of the long bar and the entry axis. A continuous bench, which snakes round the sides of the space, has been designed with spines of wood corresponding to the curvature of the back.

Other nearby works by Beth Galí are the interior of the Indumentaria clothing store on the Carrer d'Avignon and the Met. room Gallery at Carrer Nou de Sant Francesc, 4. Inaugurated in spring 2000 with an exhibit by the Dutch team MVRDR, the architecture exhibition space is below her office.

ADDRESS Plaça Reial, 8
METRO L3 Liceu or Drassanes BUS 14, 38, 59
ACCESS open

Elisabeth Galí 2000

Elisabeth Galí 2000

Bar Royale

Bar Royale hosted the launch party for Pedro Almodovar's Oscar-winning film *Everything about my Mother*, one of few Spanish films to make use of the photogenic qualities of Barcelona. This bar and lounge on two levels is located on a street between the Plaça Reial and Carrer Escudellers. The space was formerly a brothel and its curving plaster-covered columns, suggesting its colourful history, have been preserved.

The café is one of the more interesting night-time haunts to have opened in the 1990s. After the wave of 'designer' bars, followed by the economic slump of 1992, the 'total design' look of the 1980s was shunned for more economic, casual, and ad hoc spaces, in line with the fashion for 1960s' and 1970s' retro. Bar Royale functions as a café during the afternoon and a bar at night; it is designed, yet intimate, offering a relaxing setting with good acoustics and ventilation. It plays on design references from the 1950s, 1960s and 1970s.

At the entrance a long bar and upholstered bench are covered with tile remnants. Some stairs lead down to a lower-level lounge space, where the walls have been padded with salmon-coloured fabric panels and lined with comfortable upholstered couches. The glass-covered ceiling and walls enhance the acoustics.

ADDRESS Carrer Nou de Zurbano, 3
METRO L3 Liceu or Drassanes
BUS 14, 38, 59, N9, N12
ACCESS open daily from 17.00

Juan Fernandez and Modesto Bagadano 1999

Ciutat Vella

Juan Fernandez and Modesto Bagadano 1999

Centre d'Art Santa Mònica

For the conversion of this seventeenth-century former convent at the end of the Ramblas, the architects superimposed a series of elements on to the existing structure. Taking advantage of the building's position, set back from the Ramblas, they added a wooden ramped deck to bring visitors to the main floor. The sidewalk coursing and the ramp convert into a spacious platform, supported on thin metal columns, that cuts into the building entrance. A metal frame projects out above the deck for night lighting. Rather than creating a pastiche or a collage of fragments that form a new whole, these abstracted pieces are jarringly contrasted with the existing structure. Juxtapositions and insertions starkly call attention to old layers and new constructions: the transparent and the opaque, heaviness and lightness, the convex, the rectilinear and the planar.

The adjacent church has been separated from the convent with an emerging party wall ending in an oblique point. The two façades form a compositional diptych. The oculus of the refaced church is an ironic rose window. In the glass-covered patio of the convent where art is displayed an inclined metal 'veil' slices the space.

In a later phase of modification, a new 4300-square-metre administration building was constructed. The entrance is through an indented void between the convent and the addition on Santa Madrona Street. It is covered by a minimalist stone canopy that juts into the street to form a giant portal.

ADDRESS La Rambla, 7
METRO L3 Drassanes
BUS 14, 38, 59
ACCESS open Monday to Saturday, 11.00–14.00, 17.00–20.00; Sunday, 11.00–15.00

Viaplana and Piñón 1985–92

Viaplana and Piñón 1985–92

El Corte Inglés

The creation of a unified façade for this department store, prominently located in Plaça Catalunya, involved the compositional skills and co-ordination of two different teams of architects. Eliés Torres and José A Martínez Lapeña had been commissioned to design a new skin for the existing Corte Inglés department store dating back to 1962 and sited mid block, its extension along the Ronda de Sant Pere and the northern corner. In 1993 MBM was commisioned to add a new building on the south corner which incorporated a modernist tribune designed by Antoni Maria Gallissà, taken from an earlier building on Carrer Fontanella. Corte Inglés acquired the building during construction. The suggestion to give the various parts and extensions a unified treatment came from city hall.

Both sets of architects treat their corners as curved volumes, though with different articulations. Torres and Martínez Lapeña cut an array of vertical windows into the stone curtain wall. The store's name stands out above the corner, as if cut out of stone. The upper-level restaurant is treated with a band of curving transparent glass and a covered terrace ending in the articulation of the elevator tower. The curve by MBM is given a horizontal reading with metal banding. Use of the same stone curtain wall and the sweeping bronze canopy at street level unify the two interventions. The building's interior courtyard by Torres and Martínez Lapeña is an abstract gridded sheet-metal brise-soleil enclosing the entire façade.

ADDRESS Plaça Catalunya, 14–16/Ronda de Sant Pere/Carrer Fontanella
METRO L1, L2, L3 Catalunya
BUS 7, 16, 22, 28, 35, 42, 47
ACCESS open

E Torres, J A Martínez Lapeña/MBM and A Puigdomènech 1990–94

E Torres, J A Martínez Lapeña/MBM and A Puigdomènech 1990–94

Palau de la Música Catalana Addition

The architect Òscar Tusquets has made two respectful interventions into one of the most emblematic modernist works in Barcelona. The original building was commissioned from Gaudí's great contemporary Lluís Domènech i Montaner in 1905 by the choral group El Orfeo Catalan, still the owners. The Palau, with its rationalist structure of brick piers and steel construction, has a vestibule and monumental stair leading to the glazed u-shaped auditorium above. Use of stained glass, mosaic, and forged iron combined natural motifs and symbols of Catalan nationalism. Inspired by Richard Wagner's concept of the *gesamtkunstwerk*, the architect orchestrated a team of sculptors and artisans in this 'total work of art', a monument to Catalan and international music and song.

Tusquets' first intervention enlarged seating capacity and partially opened the site to the north-west by demolishing part of a neighbouring church. A chamber-music hall, a new entrance lobby and stairway were added, and an administration wing whose circular turret can be seen from Via Laietana. The apartment where Lluís Millet, founder of the choral group, lived was made into a library. Located directly above the stage, Millet could look down and listen to the concerts below through an oculus, now covered with glass. The church has been completely demolished, revealing the finished longitudinal façade. A new adjacent building is planned to house a boutique, a restaurant and other facilities.

ADDRESS Plaça d'Amadeu Vives, 1/Carrer de Sant Pere Més Alt, 11
METRO L4 Urquinaona
BUS 16, 17, 19, 45
ACCESS tours in English are organised by the Palau and by the Route of Modernisme

Òscar Tusquets and Carles Díaz 1982–90, 2000

Ciutat Vella

Òscar Tusquets and Carles Díaz 1982–90, 2000

Picasso Museum Renovation

Every year more than one million people contemplate Picasso's connection with Barcelona within this series of interconnected gothic palaces. The artist spent his early life in Barcelona and held his first exhibition in the El Quatre Gats Café. His father taught at the Art Academy in the nearby Llotja building. When Picasso moved to Paris he left a portfolio of early work with a friend which he presented as a gift to the city in 1973; the city initially took over two medieval palaces to house the work. The sheer quantity of visitors has spawned successive enlargements, the first in 1982 by Jordi Garcés with Enric Sòria. With this latest addition, the museum occupies five palaces on one of the most beautiful and emblematic streets in the city.

The Carrer de Montcada in the Ribera neighbourhood has become a cultural axis of museums and galleries; and many other institutions occupy palaces, their courtyards open to passers-by. Dating back to the twelfth century, it was a *vilanova*, a new development created to connect the maritime quarter with the commercial sector. By the fourteenth century it was the grandest street in the city. The current enlargement was inaugurated on 26 October 1999 when the Casa Mauri and the Finestres Palace were added to the Meca, Berenguer d'Aguilar and the Baró de Castellet palaces, increasing the space from 7144 to 10,628 square metres.

Scale and luminosity are the key characteristics of the new intervention. Though enormous, the spaces are handled as discreet modern containers that leave the art to make the statements. Clean and light, they are a response to the museum's modern technical requirements. Functional elements such as metal security doors add a modern language. Windows provide diffuse light.

A new interior street, open to all, was created on the ground floor

Jordi Garcés 1999

Jordi Garcés 1999

Picasso Museum Renovation

which unites the palaces and gives access to the bar, restaurant, the newly enlarged boutique, and an auditorium, which has its own garden, a space of archaeological interest where medieval remains are exposed. In one of the first-floor halls the ceiling paintings date back to the thirteenth century.

ADDRESS Carrer de Montcada, 15 and 23
METRO L4 Jaume I
BUS 16, 17, 19, 45
ACCESS Tuesday to Saturday, 10.00–20.00; Sunday, 10.00–15.00

Jordi Garcés 1999

Jordi Garcés 1999

Homage to Picasso

When Barcelona City Council commissioned Antoni Tàpies, the most important Catalan artist of his generation, to commemorate the centennial of Pablo Picasso's birth and to remodel the avenue that bears the latter's name, he went against the conventions of traditional monuments and open-air sculptures. Tàpies enclosed his sculpture, a collage of old furniture, graffitied sheets and steel beams, within a 4-metre x 4-metre x 4-metre glass cube. Marking the exact centre of the Passeig de Picasso, the work forms part of a canal fountain by the architects Roser Amadó and Lluís Domènech that flows the length of the street at the edge of the Ciutadella Park. It can be found directly in front of the 'Shade House', a wooden lath structure by Fontserè, designer of the park.

The view of the objects scattered within Tàpies' glass cube is distorted by the streams of water that pour out over the box. The beams are strong structuring elements that not only hold up the roof but also hide the water tubes. This unconventional fountain is an anti-monument, homage to the irreverent, non-conformist and anti-aesthetic Picasso. Graffitied on the sheet covering the sofa and other remnants of bourgeois furnishings are quotes from Picasso, who once called painting 'a sum of destructions'. Hand-written by Tàpies on the cloth are Picasso's declarations: 'When I don't have blue I use red', 'What saves me is doing it worse everyday' and 'No, painting is not done to decorate apartments, but is a weapon of war used offensively and defensively against the enemy'.

ADDRESS Passeig de Picasso
METRO L1 Arc de Triomf or L4 Jaume I
BUS 39, 51, 40, 41, 42, 141
ACCESS open

Antoni Tàpies 1983

Antoni Tàpies 1983

Eixample

Fundació Tàpies

Appearing above the street are the swirling wires of a sculptural drawing that hovers over the three-storey modernist building below. The work is Catalan artist Antoni Tàpies' *Chair and Cloud* and it is set over the art foundation that bears his name. The centre is dedicated to contemporary art exhibitions and occupies the renovated former Montaner i Simon publishing house, designed by the great proponent of rational modernism, Lluís Domènech i Montaner, in 1879. This early project, built for the architect's family business, was the first industrial workshop type in the largely residential Eixample district.

The current foundation was brought into being through an accord between the city and Tàpies and his family – the latter would donate art works and a library, and manage the centre; the public sector would provide the building and funding for the renovation.

In transforming the building from a place of work and storage to a place for the public display of art, the architects sought to enhance and modernise its spatial qualities. They have exploited the structure's high spaces, slender cast-iron columns and beams, natural illumination and the wooden shelving of the printing area on the upper floor, which now functions as the library.

The semi-basement level was chosen as the most important floor because of its flexibility in accommodating changing exhibitions. Upon entering, the three-storey space provides a perspective of the entire building made up of three layers: a zone contiguous with the street containing the reception and bookstore; an extensive sky-lit internal floor for exhibitions; and a backyard raised garden that is accessed via a triangular staircase of cream coloured stone. This walled space offers a place of rest and brings in diffuse light. A new basement added exhibition space. The great skylight was modified to admit only northern light. Against this

Roser Amadó and Lluís Domènech 1986–90

Roser Amadó and Lluís Domènech 1986–90

industrial shell, the designers have added various stairs with a new vocabulary of materials.

Tàpies' crowning wire sculpture is supported on a metal structure that rectifies the height change between the foundation and the five-storey adjoining buildings, by hiding the view of the party walls with a series of metal screen supports.

ADDRESS Carrer d'Aragó, 255
METRO L3, L5 Passeig de Gràcia
BUS 7, 16, 17, 22, 24, 28, 43
ACCESS open Tuesday to Sunday, 10.00–20.00

Roser Amadó and Lluís Domènech 1986–90

Roser Amadó and Lluís Domènech 1986–90

B.d.

This design store occupies the semi-basement level of an historic modernist building, the Casa Thomas by Lluís Domènech i Montaner. With the creation of B.d. in 1972, the architects of Studio PER – Òscar Tusquets, Lluís Clotet, Pep Bonet, and Cristian Cirici – launched themselves not just as designers, but also as manufacturers and retailers of their own products: furnishings, objects and fittings, as well as replicas of historic designs by Gaudí, Terragni and Mackintosh. They sold modern classics and made new editions of others; they risked producing works that no one else would manufacture at the time.

This helped mark the re-emergence of design in Barcelona. Demands from the domestic market for new local design coincided with the advent of democracy, an emphasis on Catalan culture, and increased prosperity. This new vitality surfaced after the long suppression of furniture, graphic and product design during the Franco era when these activities were considered subversive due to their relation to regional identity. With few exceptions, by the 1940s and '50s local designs were not being manufactured; foreign products were simply copied more cheaply. Studio PER's design activities helped to remedy this situation. B.d's wire-mesh bench, the 'Banco Catalano', their apartment mailboxes and transparent plastic air extractor have become classics of Catalan design. Their work played with a wide range of post-modern influences and Tusquet's friendship with Salvador Dalí led to the production of the artist's surrealist lamps, love seat, and door handle.

B.d.'s shop renovation was an innovative intervention in a historic building. The Thomas house (1895–98), like the Montàner i Simon Publishing building, now the Fundació Tàpies (see page 2.2), was an unusual type for the Eixample. Originally a two-storey industrial workshop with a semi-basement floor, it housed a graphic-arts business until

Studio PER 1979

Studio PER 1979

B.d.

1973. Three apartment floors were added on to it in 1912 by Fransesc Guardia with Domènech's approval. The large double-height arched window with iron grille is protected by a glass front. The levels split into two spaces – store below, display above. A skylight in the interior courtyard illuminates the store from within.

ADDRESS Carrer de Mallorca, 291–293
METRO L3, L5 Diagonal
BUS 20, 43, 44
ACCESS open

Studio PER 1979

Studio PER 1979

Vinçon

By the time that cultural changes and economic prosperity precipitated the Barcelona design boom of the 1970s and 1980s, Fernando Amat's houseware and furniture store on Passeig de Gràcia was already a landmark. He had been at the forefront since the 1960s, becoming influential in design when he took over his father's German porcelain shop, which dated back to the 1940s. Neither designer nor manufacturer himself, the merchandise Amat chose was guided by personal criteria and love of objects, rather than marketing studies. In fact, Amat created the market, with a sensibility for objects ranging from haute design to beautiful anonymous everyday objects from around the world. He might be compared to Terence Conran, though Vinçon has never become a chain.

The Sala Vinçon gallery located in the store showcased young local designers, providing a forum and support for their work. Exhibitions included tables by Bigas Luna, the artist turned film-maker, in 1973, Javier Mariscal's 'Amoral Furniture' in 1981, and Òscar Tusquets' Gaulino chair of 1987 which fused design characteristics from Gaudí and Carlo Molino.

The store, which extends from Passeig de Gràcia to Pau Claris Street, is just doors away from Gaudí's Casa Milà where Amat lives. It occupies two levels of an Eixample building, which preserves cast-iron columns on its ground floor. European and Spanish furniture is located in the sumptuous apartment once owned by modernist painter Ramon Casas and a former residence of the playwright, journalist and artist Santiago Rusinyol. Lawn and outdoor furnishings are displayed on the enormous terrace in the centre of the block.

The shop can itself be considered as an evolving design proposition. Long known for interesting window design, great care is also taken in

Fernando Amat 1967–99

Fernando Amat 1967–99

Vinçon

the merchandise layout, lighting and the display of objects ranging from wheelbarrows, rakes, and bird calls to the latest in European re-editions. Amat 's special interest in graphic design led him to commission the North-American artist Barbara Kruger to create a shopping bag that read 'I shop therefore I am'.

ADDRESS Passeig de Gràcia, 96
METRO L3 Diagonal
BUS 22, 28, T2, 100, 101
ACCESS open

Fernando Amat 1967–99

Fernando Amat 1967–99

La Pedrera: Espai Gaudí

This tour of Gaudí's architecture guides the visitor through some of the most spectacular spaces that he designed. The Espai Gaudí is a permanent installation created by Daniel Giralt-Miracle and Fernando Marzá that gives visitors access to the recently restored attic and roof terrace. In the diaphanous curving space of undulating brick parabolic arches a series of models and audiovisuals explains Gaudí's universe to the visitor. The route leads to the stepping landscape above, and then to a typical apartment below.

Casa Milà was Gaudí's last large-scale work before he dedicated himself solely to Sagrada Familia. Popularly known as 'La Pedrera' or the stone quarry, the building demonstrates an innovative treatment of an Eixample corner plot, bringing light in with two curving courtyards and using columns as structure. In contrast to all the buildings around it that use a structure of rectilinear interior walls, the columns allow for a proto-free plan. All the room divisions are formed of organic curving partitions, following the premise that there are no straight lines in nature. The columnar structure permits different apartment divisions on every floor. The plan to crown the building with a 12-metre-high statue of the Virgin Mary was rejected by the owners. Ramps that would have allowed tenants to drive up to their apartments weren't built either. But this work demonstrates the expressionistic collaboration of Josep Maria Jujol, who designed the seaweed balconies, courtyard murals and roof terrace.

Restoration began in 1988 with the courtyards and patios when the original colours and textures of the paintings, and the stone and ceramic details were determined. Work was resumed in 1991, coordinated by Enric Mira with the art historian Raquel Lacuesta, with the aim of opening the attic's dramatic spaces to the public. To accomplish this, the fine 1950s-style apartments built there by Barba Corsini were torn out.

Francisco Javier Asarta and Robert Brufau 1991–96

Francisco Javier Asarta and Robert Brufau 1991–96

La Pedrera: Espai Gaudí

Most arches had to be rebuilt since they had lost rows of bricks during the conversion. The structure was consolidated and elements that had been added were removed. At an earlier date, the Caixa, the building's owner, converted the city's first subterranean car park into an auditorium space. The main level is an exhibition gallery run by the bank where some of the more elaborate plaster ceilings can be seen. La Pedrera was designated a World Heritage site by UNESCO.

ADDRESS Passeig de Gràcia, 92/Carrer de Provença, 261–265
METRO L3, L5 Diagonal
BUS 22, 24, 28, T2
ACCESS open daily, 10.00–20.00

Francisco Javier Asarta and Robert Brufau 1991–96

Eixample

Francisco Javier Asarta and Robert Brufau 1991–96

Tragaluz

Once an affluent single-family home, this project for a bar and restaurant began with the roof. The 'Tragaluz' or skylight is actually a sloping glass roof that completely covers the top of the original house and gains space for the restaurant that has been structured on various levels. The glass panels between the metal structure can slide open and be shaded automatically with wooden blinds.

The building houses two different eating areas: the ground-floor foyer and bar lead to a more casual fast-eating area known as 'Tragarapid'. The elegant 'Tragaluz' beneath the glass roof above offers diners a more sophisticated menu. The designer Pep Cortés, known for his bar and shop interiors, collaborated with Javier Mariscal, who provided the graphics and logo for the menu and signage. This is only one of many such collaborations in interior-design projects by the Valencian-born comic-strip artist and designer, and author of the Olympic mascot Cobi.

Under the skylight, murals by Isabel Esteva give warmth to the space, which contrasts comfort and modernity, baroque and functionalism. The palate of materials combines rich woods and metals. The character and materials of the stair change as it ascends, passing by the metal-mesh cylinder coat room on the ground floor. It reaches the summit in a circular staircase surrounding an artificial tree trunk under the roof.

ADDRESS Passatge de la Concepció, 5
METRO L3, L5 Diagonal
BUS 22, 24, 28 T2, N4
ACCESS open daily, 13.30–16.00, 20.30–24.00 (Thursday to Saturday until 1.00)

Pepe Cortés 1989–90

Eixample

Pepe Cortés 1989–90

Nick Havanna

The designer-bar trend began in Barcelona in the 1980s and subsequently spread to other cities. It was a tendency that forged collaborations between practitioners and lead to fusions of architecture, interior design, art, fashion, and graphics. Some of the main figures who emerged were Eduardo Samsó, Alfredo Arribas and Javier Mariscal, the underground comic-strip artist and graphic and furniture designer.

Designer bars acted as ephemeral night-time counterpoints to the public spaces and plazas created in the same years. They responded to the newly acquired consumer power of Spanish youth and to their inclination to meet socially outside the family home. In the ritual of 'la marcha', groups of friends move from one bar to another during the course of the evening. Even though today these bars may seem like period pieces, they reflect formal innovation and play as well as interesting use of materials and details and 'typical' Spanish images.

Nick Havanna was a fictional Cuban cowboy whose character was the inspiration behind the ambience of the bar. This coolly lit space, which has the scale of a discothèque, reveals some of the design techniques used by Samsó in other projects including clothing shops such as Jean Pierre Bua (1984) on Avinguda Diagonal that coincided with the boom in Spanish fashion. His strategy was to create a neutral space and dramatically highlight certain elements with lighting. These were treated like jewels – theatrically lit, they created a sense of artifice, a display of rich materials against a stark backdrop.

Samsó has created different settings for different stages of the evening at Nick Havanna. In the entry area, the long bar is covered in cowhide and lined by chrome-based stools with leather sling seats. A grid of suspended television sets at the edge of a large square space may be viewed from concrete bleacher seating. A pendulum swings in the centre beside

Eduardo Samsó 1985

Eduardo Samsó 1985

Eixample

2.22

tables and chairs designed by Philippe Starck (whose furniture was initially produced in Barcelona by Disform). Samsó was the first to treat washrooms as privileged, provocative spaces, integral to nocturnal experience. The men's room urinal is a waterfall cascading down.

In the 1980s camp and stylised play with 'typical' Spanish images was a cultural tendency extending from furniture and interior design to fashion and film, as seen in Samso's Bregado sofa designed to mimic the body of a bull; Pedro Almodovar's movies *Matador*, or *Woman on the verge of a nervous breakdown* (in which gazpacho laced with sedatives puts the ensemble actors to sleep), or Bigas Luna' *Jamon Jamon*, where a serrano hambone served as a weapon, and the highway billboards with a bull silhouette for Osborne brandy acted as backdrops.

Eixample

ADDRESS Carrer de Rosselló, 208
METRO L5 Diagonal FCG Provença
BUS 7, 16, 17, 31, 6, 15, 33, 34
ACCESS open Sunday to Thursday, 23.00–4.00; Friday and Saturday, 23.00–5.00

Eduardo Samsó 1985

Eixample

Eduardo Samsó 1985

Velvet

Alfredo Arribas became one of the most important designers of night-time Barcelona in the 1980s. His bars were sensual, visually dynamic, and full of changing spatial sequences. Celebrating youth culture, these totally designed spaces included specially created logos and furniture. Bathrooms took on an importance equal to that of any other space. Lighting was used to highlight, dramatise and enhance. As his work became more flamboyant and extravagant, it toyed with an ever-wider range of influences: visual jokes, 1950s interiors, Spanish cultural clichés such as bull-fighting and flamenco, film noir and US post-apocalyptic movies such as *Blade Runner*. The latter inspired his metal-coated Network Café, a collaboration with Eduard Samsó, where the positioning of television screens forced diners to glance across each others' tables.

Arribas' bars and restaurants were often designed around themes: Gambrinus, a café at the port, was capped with a giant prawn by Mariscal. At Louie Vega, near Tarragona, the crash of a fictional pilot fuelled the design. But they have nothing in common with the later US trend for theme restaurants.

David Lynch's 1987 film *Blue Velvet* provided the name and inspiration for the eerie plush-velvet ambience and rich colours of this ground-floor bar. The furniture and chairs recall Italian architect Carlo Molino's erotic 1940s' and '50s' designs. A reaction against the cold aloofness of Samso's Nick Havanna bar, this club is smaller and more intimate. It has an exotic lounge feeling, starting with the metal entry ramp outside.

ADDRESS Carrer de Balmes, 161
METRO L5 Diagonal FGC Provença
BUS 7, 16, 17, 31, 6, 15, 33, 34
ACCESS open

Alfredo Arribas 1987

Alfredo Arribas 1987

Zsa Zsa

This ground-floor bar was conceived of as a box within a box: different surfaces have been built out from the existing container. The floor is floating wood parquet; the false ceiling leaves a gap for service installations and recessed lighting. Glass walls are built out from the lateral sides of the existing enclosure to form thin storage zones. On one side, the stock of liquor bottles is displayed behind transparent glass. On the other, wood veneers line the back of the glass, creating a hidden storage area and acting as a giant light screen. The building's stair volume invades the space and is covered by Oriental carpets to improve the acoustics of the otherwise hard surfaces.

The highlight of the design is the programmed sequence of six different lighting effects that change the mood of the bar. Alternately over the course of the evening the glass walls become reflective mirrors, light sources or vitrines. Industrially produced stailes-steel restaurant trays have been transformed into tables and ceiling sconces.

Eixample

ADDRESS Carrer de Rosselló, 156
METRO L5 Diagonal FCG Provença
BUS 7, 16, 17, 31, 67, 68
ACCESS open

Daniel Freixes and Vicente Miranda 1988

Daniel Freixes and Vicente Miranda 1988

Lawyers Mutual of Catalunya HQ

Though less well-known internationally than many of his peers, Carles Ferrater has a wide ranging practice, characterised by inventiveness and fine detailing. He is the author of the Botanical Garden in Montjuic, the Juan Carlos Hotel and spa and the new congress centre on the Diagonal, as well as many apartment buildings and houses. His work reveals an exploration of types, the articulation of elegant slender geometrical volumes, and a Mediterranean sense of abstraction.

This project in the Eixample won a 1999 FAD prize for interior design. It involved the radical transformation of commercial premises into a headquarters for the Lawyers Mutual, in an extremely deep site with an irregular perimeter. A three-storey central space has been excavated out of the original ground floor and basement. This voided space connects the medical offices below with the ground-floor entry area and a suspended gangway mezzanine that serves as the office archives. Circulation elements, stairs and a ramp link the reception and work zones.

The project emphasises the longitudinal perspective of the space with black slate floors, white walls and geometric furnishings. A giant glass window opens the interior to the street. The 50-metre-deep site had no back garden façade or illumination. In the back of the site, a new interior courtyard with plants brings natural light to the administration and meeting rooms.

ADDRESS Carrer Roger de Llúria, 106–108
CLIENT Mutua de Previsión Social de los Abogados de Catalunya
METRO L4 Girona
BUS 20, 39, 45, 47
ACCESS open

Carles Ferrater, Joan Guilbernau, and Elena Mateu 1999

Eixample

Carles Ferrater, Joan Guilbernau, and Elena Mateu 1999

Pati de les Aigües

The Water Tower courtyard, public park and children's swimming pool is one of the few interior block spaces in the Eixample open for public use, which was the original intention of Catalan engineer Ildefons Cerdà's masterplan for the city's expansion laid out in 1859. The 550 new blocks proposed were to have public gardens and a variety of residential configurations. Cerdà drew up perimeter-block schemes, bar buildings that were open at the ends, and small mews streets that cut the scale of the blocks in two. This variation in the grid also accounted for a range of housing types, from private homes for the wealthy to workers' housing.

The low green city envisioned by Cerdà never happened – privatisation claimed the interiors of the blocks. As a result, anyone in the Eixample will notice the lack of public space. The city administration and the ProEixample organisation now seek to reclaim some of the interiors for public use. This publicly financed project predates the current effort.

Entered through a passageway in an exterior building, the park with its grid of trees frames an old water tower. Retained by the city as a monument to urban memory, the tower is the main focus of the space. It is surrounded by a curving shallow pool that acts as a children's swimming area in the summer. The enclosing walls of the park have been lined with marble fragments, connoting paving patterns and updating *trencadi*s, the collaging of broken fragments so common in modernist works.

ADDRESS Carrer de Roger de Llúria between Carrer del Consell de Cent and Diputació
METRO L4 Girona
BUS 39, 45, 47
ACCESS open

Carme Ribas and Andreu Arriola 1987

Eixample

Carme Ribas and Andreu Arriola 1987

Port Vell

Moll de la Fusta

This was the first area involved in the revitalisation of the city's water-front, linking Barcelona again to the sea. Although the city's history had long been intimately linked to maritime activities, different structures had closed in and isolated the port. This linear space running between the Ramblas and the Via Laietana on the Bosch i Alsina pier, popularly known as the 'Wooden Pier' or Moll de la Fusta, was given over to the public, once the port authority had accepted the change of use in 1982. The port train line and large-scale warehouses were removed and the highway was partially sunken beneath a raised pedestrian platform.

The project confronts various layers and sectional differences between the water's edge and the street level making visual connections to the sea. From the port, a palm-tree-lined, cobbled pedestrian promenade along the water's edge has been set adjacent to a local-traffic service lane. From there, the sunken highway has been covered with a stone-faced construction forming a raised promenade at the level of Passeig de Colom. A series of pavilions with curved laminated wooden roof beams emerges from the stone section. Two footbridges provide the only access from the Moll de la Fusta to the lower port level.

After an initial euphoric reception, with the subsequent opening of other promenades and the Maremagnum (see page 3.6) that are more directly connected to the water, the bars along this strip have mostly closed down and the space seems somewhat abandoned.

ADDRESS Moll de la Fusta, Passeig de Colom
METRO L3 Drassanes or L4 Barceloneta
BUS 14, 16, 17, 18, 36, 45, 57, 59, 64
ACCESS open

Manuel de Solà-Morales 1983–87

Manuel de Solà-Morales 1983–87

Barcelona Head

Marking the end of Via Laietana and the intersection of Moll de la Fusta, Port Vell, and the Espanya and Dipòsit Piers, this artwork commissioned by the city government to enhance Barcelona's waterfront is sited on a triangular inclined plane designed by Pedro Barragan. The prominent site is practically at the entrance to the seafront ring road, the Barceloneta neighbourhood and the Maremagnum commercial centre (see page 3.6). With the opening up of Barcelona to the sea, it is now possible to walk for kilometres along the waterfront from the Columbus statue to the beach at the city's Besòs river limit. This is only one of the many sculptural works set along this promenade.

Barcelona Head is representative of the late work of Roy Lichtenstein, the American pop artist who became famous in the 1960s for his flat, blown-up images of comic strips. This is a cut-out graphic work rather than a sculpture in the round. It forms part of a series of sculpture heads by the artist that are called 'brushstrokes' for the cartoon-like brushwork that form the features of the face. Screen dots, mimicking enlargements of offset-print material, have been created with ceramic pieces. *Trencadis* (broken ceramic mosaics) were used to carry out the rest.

ADDRESS Passeig de Colom, Moll d'Espanya, Via Laietana
METRO L4 Jaume I or Barceloneta I
BUS 14, 36, 57, 59, 64, 157
ACCESS open

Roy Lichtenstein 1992

Roy Lichtenstein 1992

Maremagnum

Maremagnum is a tourist attraction that creates a continuous promenade from the city out to the sea on the Espanya Pier. This private post-Olympic development receives 18 million visitors a year, more than Euro-Disney, and is representative of the transformation from maritime workplace to leisure space that has occurred on many waterfronts since the 1970s.

With its IMAX theatre, aquarium, multi-screen cinema, shopping centre, food court, mini golf, games arcade, restaurants and discothèques, it is an American model reinterpreted by a Catalan cultural filter with its emphasis on uninterrupted public space. As an enclave it is a compact generic complex that could be anywhere, except that here it has been carefully adapted to local urban conditions. Connecting to the major arteries of the historic centre, the pier continues out from the Ramblas with the wood-decked footbridge, the Rambla del Mar, and from the Via Laietana with the Ismuth park. With its link to the urban ring road it also forms part of a citywide network.

As one of the first such private commercial developments in the city it was highly contentious. Debates ranged from the privatisation of public space to theme parking and spectacularisation. Members of the architectural community criticised the complex for blocking views to the sea. However, since its inauguration in 1995 it has become fully integrated with the city.

The high level of design is to the credit of the architects who created the masterplan, the Parc de l'Istme (1990–92) and designed the Rambla del Mar leading out to the 37,000-square-metre commercial centre on the pier with 24,000 square metres of parking space below. They conceived of the Maremagnum as a dock over a dock. Public spaces of varied scale and ambience link up the different entertainment complexes between scattered sculptural lighting elements, pergolas and other urban

Viaplana and Piñón 1990–95

Viaplana and Piñón 1990–95

3.8

furnishings. The 3000-square-metre Parc de l'Istme is a grass-covered hill cut by retaining walls that separate vehicular and pedestrian circulation. A brick pathway leads to a wooden boardwalk plaza that inclines up over the road to underground parking. The balustrade forms a long continuous bench with a granite seat.

The Maremagnum commercial centre has been treated as a wide interior street set into a low square volume with concrete columns. At the building entrance from the Rambla del Mar, a convex mirrored-glass surface curves upward from the doors to the roof, capturing and distorting the reflections of visitors and the sea like a fun-house mirror. The façade facing the city is lined by two levels of exterior porticoes and walkways that provide outdoor seating for the restaurants and bars along it. On the interior, shops have continuous glass façades on two levels with an elevator set to the edge of a metal-panelled ceiling that tapers upwards to a sky-lit roof. The Plaça de l'Odisea borders the other entrance façade and opens an axis with views from the historic centre to the industrial clock pier.

Port Vell

ADDRESS Moll d'Espanya
METRO L3 Drassanes or L4 Barceloneta
BUS 14, 36, 38, 57, 59, 64, 157
ACCESS open

Viaplana and Piñón 1990–95

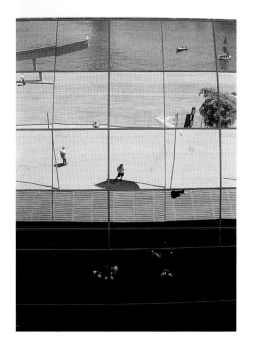

Viaplana and Piñón 1990–95

Rambla de Mar

The Rambla is an urban space of passage, movement and linkage with light sculptural elements. This maritime footbridge is set slightly off-centre to the Plaça del Portal de la Pau and the Columbus statue which marks the end of the 2-kilometre-long historic Ramblas. This pedestrian space, part bridge, boardwalk and plaza, extends the Ramblas into the port and links it to the commercial and recreational complex of the Mare-magnum (see page 3.6) on the Moll d'Espanya by the same architects.

A direct, straight route has been inscribed into the boardwalk, high-lighted above by curved beams set over metal supports. These steel waves mark the route to the new enclave and have night lighting incorporated into the design. The boardwalk also curves upward like a wave to form a drawbridge. It was thought of as a 'wooden beach' by the architects. Over its 40-metre route it flares in and out to create curved zones for rest, fitted with benches and free-standing glass panels framed in metal that block the wind and protect strollers.

ADDRESS Moll de les Drassanes
METRO L3 Drassanes
BUS 14, 36, 38, 57, 59, 64, 157
ACCESS open

Viaplana and Piñón 1993–94

Viaplana and Piñón 1993–94

IMAX Cinema

Most IMAX theatres – cinemas with technology for large-format, three-dimensional and panoramic films – are set in theme parks and treated as 'ducks'. A 'duck' to use Robert Venturi's description is, for instance, a doughnut-shaped building where doughnuts are sold. Most IMAX cinemas take their form from science-fiction themes and wear space-age dress. In this case, though the dimensions and layout of the screening area were completely determined by the technology, the architects have opted for a dignified and quiet volumetric urban building rather than a fantasy billboard.

Entered from a plaza at the end of the Ismuth Park, a white prismatic volume of lacquered aluminum panels in horizontal bands emerges from a trapezoidal granite plinth. This horizontal base contains the entrance and a bar on the ground floor and a restaurant and offices above. The white volume corresponds to the theatre. The double-height foyer is sky-lit and marked off by curving brick walls set above concrete columns. They separate the bar to the left from the ticket office and screening room to the right. The public drinking and dining areas have horizontal glazing with a view of the port.

The spherical IMAX technology determined the form of the container, and the incline of the seats and colours were givens. The screening room is fitted with two large screens, one fixed and the other hinged and entered from restaurant level.

ADDRESS Moll d'Espanya
METRO L3 Drassanes or L4 Barceloneta
BUS 14, 19, 36, 40, 57, 59, 64
ACCESS open 11.00–22.30 (24.15 at weekends)

Jordi Garcés and Enric Sòria 1994–95

Port Vell

Jordi Garcés and Enric Sòria 1994–95

L'Aquàrium de Barcelona

Like the nearby IMAX cinema (see page 3.12), this trapezoidal building has a highly specialised programme with determinant needs. The size of the area required for maintenance and filtering water is roughly equal to that needed for the public's itinerary. The building deals with its own dichotomy: a seaside attraction with views to the water and a windowless space where aquatic life is on view. A tremendous amount of space is given over to outdoor public areas.

From a continuous line of green slate stairs visitors enter an enormous triangular hypostile court covered by a concrete slab, with ticket pavilions and an entrance to the store. Before entering the aquarium area, the route ramps down on wooden plank walkways through a double-height glazed greenhouse overlooking the water and planted with hundreds of exotic species of bamboo.

The aquarium's most spectacular feature and the main organising element of the interior is the Oceanarium, a cylindrical tank with a 38-metre diameter, carved into by 80 metres of transparent tunnels. After passing 20 aquaria of different sizes, visitors enter the glass tunnels while sharks and other sea creatures swim over their heads. The route is complemented by educational spaces: an auditorium and two classrooms for lectures and audiovisuals. On the uppermost level of the building the cylinder emerges as a sky-lit temporary exhibition space surrounded by a roof deck and a cafeteria that takes full advantage of the views from the glass perimeter, and a children's interactive discovery area.

ADDRESS Moll d'Espanya
METRO L3 Drassanes or L4 Barceloneta
BUS 14, 19, 36, 38, 39, 40, 57, 59, 64, 91
ACCESS open 9.30–21.00; September and weekends, 9.30–21.30

Esteve Terradas and Robert Terradas 1992–95

Esteve Terradas and Robert Terradas 1992–95

World Trade Center

This pier complex by the American architects known for the Louvre pyramid is one of the few developments along the waterfront dedicated to business activities instead of leisure and consumption. The building was received like a foreign invader: an American corporate model in Catalan waters. Completion took more than a decade and it is now completely taken over by internet start-ups.

Built at the end of the pier, to one side of the Maremagnum (see page 3.6), the centre is composed of a circular volume of buildings inscribed into a square base. This volume in turn has been cut with a square void that forms a central plaza. It has been sculpted into four tapering buildings with slightly curved forms. In scale and massing they make a facile allusion to the ocean liners docked near by.

The waterfront centre includes offices, a congress centre and a hotel. It is one of 327 World Trade Centers around the world in 100 countries, based on the concept and organisation developed in 1968 by Guy Tozzoly with the objective of promoting international business ventures and facilitating the clustering of companies. With 40,000 square metres of office space, individual spaces offer a minimum of 40 square metres. Shared spaces include an auditorium for 430 people and 30 meeting rooms. Companies have access to services such as simultaneous translation, secretarial and receptionist pools, copy services, audiovisual materials, and the internet. The project includes a commercial zone in the ground floor, underground parking for 1000 cars and 1200 square metres of exhibition space as well as two international maritime stations.

The offices are grouped around a porticoed public plaza with a scenographic fountain bordered by the two levels and terraces of the Congress Center. The office buildings include a basement, ground floor and seven levels of offices, with installations above. The top floor has a terrace that

I M Pei, Cobb, Freed & Partners 1989–99

I M Pei, Cobb, Freed & Partners 1989–99

3.18

projects out to sea like the prow of a boat. The materials are 10-centimetre-thick concrete panels and horizontal aluminium windows with blue-green glass.

Like the nearby Maremagnum (see page 3.6), the World Trade Center continues the density of the city into the port. While playing with maritime allusions these complexes actually close in the waterfront and urbanise it.

Port Vell

ADDRESS Moll de Barcelona
METRO L3 Drassanes
BUS 38, 14, 36, 57, 59, 64, 157
ACCESS open

I M Pei, Cobb, Freed & Partners 1989–99

Port Vell

I M Pei, Cobb, Freed & Partners 1989–99

Moll de la Barceloneta

The Barceloneta neighbourhood, a colony formed of narrow north–south-running streets, was built in 1753 by military engineers when Philip V laid siege to the city and constructed the Ciutadella. The view of the port was traditionally blocked by customs and shipping buildings until this project opened it up. Financed by the Port Authority and municipal planning department, a kilometre-long public waterfront promenade is bordered by Passeig de Joan de Borbó, the Moll del Dipòsit and Moll Rellotge. The space begins at the warehouses now known as Palau de Mar. It is filled with bicycles, skaters, scooters, and strollers.

This long space has been built up from inflected, tapered, and folded ground planes, embankments and lines of steps. Trees were planted in a line at the street edge over a continuous paving of artificial stone. The space opens up near the water with a change in scale where scattered groupings of trees create patches of shade. Palm trees and high lighting form rhythmic markings. At the end closest to the quay, two large triangular black cobblestone slopes incline upwards to the water's edge, ending at a long line of steps down to the docks.

The same architects created the promenade's continuation along Barceloneta's coast on the other side of the Passeig de Joan de Borbó where the triangular Plaça del Mar opens out to the sea.

ADDRESS Passeig de Joan de Borbó, Moll de la Barceloneta
METRO L4 Barceloneta
BUS 14, 16, 17, 39, 45, 57, 59, 64
ACCESS open

Olga Tarrasó, Jordi Henrich, Rafael de Cáceres 1991–93

Olga Tarrasó, Jordi Henrich, Rafael de Cáceres 1991–93

Sant Sebastià Municipal Swimming Pool

This municipal swimming complex occupies the beachfront site at the end of the Barceloneta neighbourhood, where the turn of the (twentieth) century San Sebastià baths once stood. It is a horizontal block of rough concrete whose only articulations are the gridding of the concrete, the awnings and eaves that cover the openings cut into the shell, the diagonal concrete gutters, and the chamfered façade along the Passeig. Glass banding visually connects indoor and outdoor pools; horizontal openings cut into the concrete container allow swimmers to look out to the horizon.

This is a durable construction of low-maintenance materials, capable of withstanding the weathering caused by the sea air and constant use. It forms a low, solid counterpoint to the tall steel funicular tower beside it.

The first phase included a ground-floor entrance, reception area and gym. Above are the dressing rooms, a three-storey-high indoor swimming pool with bleachers and a fronton court (for playing pelota). The long-span structure covering the pool is formed of laminated wood trusses whose curving side faces downward. Blue cement blocks face the enclosing wall with glass openings below. A second phase added an outdoor pool on an elevated terrace or 'ceramic beach', 4 metres above the sand, and a solarium. Later additions will include new outdoor and indoor pools, the relocation of changing rooms and gym, and windsurfing areas along the beach.

ADDRESS Plaça del Mar
METRO L4 Barceloneta
BUS 17, 39, 64
ACCESS open with day admission

Elíes Torres and José A Martínez Lapeña 1992–95

Port Vell

Elíes Torres and José A Martínez Lapeña 1992–95

Wounded Star

The German artist Rebecca Horn became known for her body apparatuses, prosthetic devices, mechanical butterflies and bird wings, painting machines and films. Around the time of the Olympics she did a series of temporary installations in some of the rooms of the Hotel Peninsular in the Barrio Chino where she had stayed when she first visited Barcelona years before. *Wounded Star* is a public work located on the beach in Barceloneta. Four rusted cubes form a balancing tower with glass openings that can be lit at night.

This work is not really representative of the delicacy of her work in general, except perhaps in its suggestion of precarious balance. It seems to be on the brink of tumbling over. The sculpture is a lighthouse beacon with an uncertain equilibrium.

ADDRESS Platja de la Barceloneta/Carrer de Meer
METRO L4 Barceloneta
BUS 17, 39, 64, 45, 57, 59, 157
ACCESS open

Rebecca Horn 1992

Rebecca Horn 1992

Hospital del Mar

Modernisation of the Hospital del Mar complex started once it was designated the official Olympic hospital. The architects had to contend with a residual macro block lacking an urban façade and the need to make a connection between two buildings from different periods – the Hospital de la Infecciosos built in 1925 and the ten-storey Neurology Institute of 1973. The two reflect widely different trends in planning. The older typology of seven parallel pavilions with a central connecting axis had been favoured for isolating infection but had the disadvantage of long corridors. The later high-rise type concentrated facilities and cut distances but eventually fell out of use due to its rigidity and lack of growth potential. The architects have added pieces to create the more adaptable typology now in fashion: a continuous mesh or grid of mid-rise buildings with interior courtyards. Exterior spaces have been landscaped.

A façade facing out to sea was constructed along the Passeig Marítim covering a new low-rise bar building skewed at an angle to the pavilions. It encloses the block with a facing of stainless-steel panels and glass banding. The once-isolated ten-storey slab straddles its roof and has been enveloped on the lower floors. Vertical cores were added and the façades refaced. The newly enclosed interior of the block has taken on a new life with gardened spaces. The entry pavilion set there, just behind the bar, is a diaphanous space of slender steel columns supporting a metal roof.

A Biomedical Research Center was designed at the same time. This occupies a site on Carrer de Trelawny, defining the macro block's last edge with a building composed of a central spine with wings.

ADDRESS Passeig Marítim, 25–29, Carrer del Gas
METRO L4 Barceloneta or Ciutadella/Villa Olímpica BUS 45, 57, 59, 157
ACCESS open

Manuel Brullet and Albert de Pineda 1989–92

Manuel Brullet and Albert de Pineda 1989–92

Ciutadella

Jaume I Barracks, Universitat Pompeu Fabra

When the Catalan regional government founded this public university at the beginning of the 1990s, its buildings were spread around the city. Departments in a rundown area of the Ramblas mixed students with locals, transforming the neighbourhood. Some classes were held at the Estació de França when the railway company moved to new premises. With the acquisition of two military buildings from the Ministry of Defence, the site of the former fish market and the Water Deposit building on the north side of Ciutadella Park, the Universitat Pompeu Fabra will have an urban campus of more than 4 hectares, conforming to the Cerdá grid.

The project involved refurbishing two former army barracks, each occupying a whole Eixample block – the Jaume I building awarded to Esteve Bonell and Josep Maria Gil in restricted competition, and the Roger de Llúria building commissioned from Martorell, Bohigas, Mackay – and an underground 'agora' linking the buildings with public spaces by Jordi Garcés and Enric Sòria. Buildings by Miralles/Tagliabue, Josep Acebillo and Juan Navarro Baldeweg are also proposed. The Water Deposit has been transformed into a library by Lluís Clotet and Ignacio Paricio.

Military engineers built the austere rectangular Jaume I courtyard building between 1874 and 1879. Its renovation as university departments presented conflicts between the existing structure and the need for small spaces. No intervention was made to the exterior of the building and the original roof tiles were reused. To accommodate the additional surface area required, the interior floor slabs were changed and mezzanine levels and new stair cores added. Technical requirements for natural lighting and ventilation were addressed. The window open-

Esteve Bonell and Josep Maria Gil 1992–96

Jaume I Barracks, Universitat Pompeu Fabra

Esteve Bonell and Josep Maria Gil 1992–96

ings of the interior courtyard's porticoes have been enlarged, changing the façade's texture.

The central courtyard is the main public space, with access to a new underground library from a sunken patio where a tower emerges. This building is faced with alternating green and white prefabricated-concrete panels and houses reading rooms and administrative offices. Part of the library is lit by cubic skylights that emerge in the courtyard.

Across the street, the recently inaugurated Roger de Llúria building by MBM transforms the same perimeter block structure with a different strategy. The central courtyard has been roofed with a vast glass-covered white space frame. Small independent office buildings have been built below it, transforming the courtyard into an interior street and plaza complete with ramps and stairs to the surrounding classrooms.

ADDRESS Carrer de Ramon Trias Fargas, 23–25
METRO L4 Ciutadella/Vil·la la Olímpica
BUS 36, 41, 71
ACCESS open

Esteve Bonell and Josep Maria Gil 1992–96

Ciutadella

Esteve Bonell and Josep Maria Gil 1992–96

Meditation Chapel

When the rector of Pompeu Fabra University invited Antoni Tàpies to create a space for reflection, the artist, a professed agnostic 'with a religious sense', began to reflect upon the idea of meditation in today's frenzied and disjointed world. His installation, combining architecture, painting, graffiti, sculpture and found objects, favours seclusion against the spectacle of the art museum. For Tàpies, it was significant that the university considered the importance of such spaces of silence. In its reliance on art as integral to meditation, the project brings to mind Mark Rothko's chapel in Houston, Texas.

The chapel is located in the Jordi Rubió i Balaquer Agora designed by Garcés and Sòria, an underground link to the campus' two renovated barracks (see page 4.2) that contains a 300-seat auditorium and an exhibition hall. A sequence of wood-clad concrete antechambers in which the project's preparatory drawings are hung provides access to the chapel and forms the path to the promised interior seclusion. Glass sliding doors inscribed with the names of the project authors open to the chapel.

The double-height meditation hall is disrupted by a steel beam with a column on top. Tàpies left this pre-existing structure, the bare concrete walls and the natural light from an upper window. Works by the artist combine textures and surfaces, reflecting his profound interest in eastern philosophy. The *Diptic de la Campana* (Bell Diptych) is the central piece, a 3-metre x 5-metre painting of symbols in black and ochre. Calligraphic strokes of a bell are outlined by the words 'samsara' and 'nirvana', alluding to the two parts of a single principle in Hindu philosophy: the earthly and the spiritual. A pointing index finger was suggested by the Japanese refrain: 'when someone points at the moon, many people only look at the finger'. Twenty-five rustic rush-bottom chairs suspended from

Antoni Tàpies 1994

Ciutadella

Antoni Tàpies 1994

Meditation Chapel

a wall like Shaker furniture are meant to suggest ascension and may be taken down by visitors. A burlap sackcloth rug occupies the centre of the floor. Finally, the sculpture *Serp i plat* (Serpent and Plate) uses banal everyday objects to recall Santa Teresa of Avila's saying: 'God moves among the saucepans'.

ADDRESS Agora Rubió Balaguer, Carrer de Ramon, Trias Fargas, 23–25
METRO L4 Ciutadella /Vil.la Olímpica
BUS 36, 41, 71
ACCESS open Monday to Friday, 13.00–15.00

Antoni Tàpies 1994

Ciutadella

Antoni Tàpies 1994

Reservoir Building Renovation

Extreme respect for the original building was the underlying principle for transforming this monumental structure into the central library of Pompeu Fabra University's Ciutadella campus. The idea was to leave the building's grand spaces to serve as a reading room, and to construct a new building for the entrance, book stacks, technical installations and administration.

The Water Deposit building (1880) was built to store and supply water to the lake, fountains and botanical species of the Ciutadella when it was converted from an army base to parkland. It was designed by Josep Fontserè i Mestres in collaboration with Josep M Cornet i Mas. Fontserè was the author of the park's masterplan, designer of its wooden lath 'Shade House', as well as the Borne market and the surrounding apartment buildings on the other side of the Ciutadella. These buildings attest to the architect's eclectic abilities. On its roof the building supported an enormous square water tank on a structure of thick, 14-metre-high parallel brick arches with barrel vaults that allude to Roman aqueducts. Supposedly, a young architecture student carried out the calculations necessary for the deposit as part of a class project. The pupil, who passed without ever having to return to class, was Antoni Gaudí.

The building was converted into an exhibition space during the Olympic period in 1988 by Ignacio Paricio, Lluís Clotet and Joan Sabater, but it subsequently stood empty for many years. This latest conversion took full advantage of the varied spaces for reading. Five skylights from the first conversion illuminate the central spaces. The intervention makes use of prefabicated-concrete elements to form discontinuous 3-metre-high mezzanine levels. which add surface area and appear as furnishings. The building has an underground connection to the Jaume 1 barracks containing a reading room. The first phase began in July 1998.

Lluís Clotet and Ignacio Paricio 1998–2000

Lluís Clotet and Ignacio Paricio 1998–2000

Reservoir Building Renovation

Finally, the architects converted the entire roof surface into a thin laminate of water, which has reduced the load from that exerted by the original water tank. This elevated reflecting pool makes reference to the building's past life while creating a surreal and dramatic landscape at the top of the building.

ADDRESS Carrer de Wellington, 50
METRO L4 Ciutadella/Vil·la Olímpica
BUS 10, 14, 41, 71, 92
ACCESS open

Lluís Clotet and Ignacio Paricio 1998–2000

Ciutadella

Lluís Clotet and Ignacio Paricio 1998–2000

Olympic Village and Port

The creation of a seaside residential neighbourhood of 2000 apartments and a recreational harbour with 734 berths was one of the essential Olympic projects, recovering the city's relationship to the sea for both leisure and dwelling purposes. The masterplan was nostalgically named Nova Icaria for the colony set up here in the nineteenth century by followers of the utopian socialist Etienne Cabet, a major influence on the Catalan engineer Cerdá. The 150-hectare site runs from the Ciutadella Park to Poble Nou and was occupied by two train lines, various obsolete industrial buildings and a sewage-treatment plant that blocked access to the beach.

The development included the recovery of the coastline, the regeneration of 4 kilometres of beaches, the creation of 43 hectares of new parks and the construction of public facilities, all commissioned from different architectural practices. The project involved a series of complex infrastructure issues: the rerouting of railway network and sewer lines for channeling rain and waste water; the construction of the sunken seaside ring road; and the continuation of the local road network. Relocations involving 157 businesses and 147 families were swiftly negotiated. Buildings were documented and then demolished. The total cost was 200 billion pesetas of which 85 billion were for infrastructure and 9245 million for the harbour. This area has subsequently been the catalyst for further developments along the coast ending in the Diagonal Mar complex at the Besòs river border.

Following the waterfront is a series of continuous parks. These permeable linear layers are formed by the seaside promenade, the sunken beltway, the local road network and blocks of housing. The masterplan dictated the open spaces and building volumes, concentrating on small details, variations and connections. The development links up with Barce-

Martorell, Bohigas, Mackay, Puigdomènech 1985–92

Martorell, Bohigas, Mackay, Puigdomènech 1985–92

loneta's waterfront promenade and continues it as far as Poble Nou. The layout extends the Cerdá grid to the sea, making Carrer de la Marina the primary axis straddled by two 44-storey towers (see page 4.20). The entire urban unit links up to the seaside beltway running between the Llobregat to the Besòs river limits.

The harbour was conceived of as a water-filled plaza with restaurants, bars and the municipal sailing school. Like the Moll de la Fusta, balconies overlook the water from the level of the city. By the sea edge a new breakwater provides views back to the urban skyline.

The housing which served the Olympic athletes for three weeks was sold off after the event. Built by private developers according to the planning guidelines, the housing blocks were commissioned from architects who had previously won FAD design prizes. Avinguda Icària, a street built in 1820 that ends in the Poble Nou cemetery, became the main boulevard of the residential complex with a central pedestrian zone. The housing blocks re-establish the Cerdá grid and introduce 'superblocks' enclosing gardens. Some individual houses and 'gateway' buildings were constructed: MBM and Puigdomènech designed a curving residential building following the rerouted railway lines around the smokestack that remains from the Folch factory; and Elíes Torres and Martinez Lapeña's curving brick apartment complex completes the axis of Avinguda Bogatell with the Plaça Tirant lo Blanc which is both enclosing yet open to the sea. Other highlights include the gateway building by Bach and Mora for the Telefonica company on Carrer de Joan Miró and Avinguda de Icària and Viaplana and Piñón's buildings at Avinguda de Icària, 174–184.

The housing projects offered heterogeneous approaches and design quality yet today this is the city's most homogeneous neighbourhood – strangely empty and uninhabited despite all the public space. Most of the

Martorell, Bohigas, Mackay, Puigdomènech 1985–92

Martorell, Bohigas, Mackay, Puigdomènech 1985–92

4.18

young professionals who live here work in other areas of the city and with its limited connection to the public transport system it functions more as a dormitory commuter area than as a real, vital neighbourhood. The fast rate of construction resulted in a series of problems which have lead to pending lawsuits in several of the buildings. Only a few years after completion some projects are already being 'restored'.

Ciutadella

ADDRESS Carrer de la Marina, Moscou, Doctor Trueta, Bogatell, Bisbe Climent, Ronda del Litoral
METRO L4 Ciutadella/Vil·la Olímpic or Bogatell
BUS 6, 36, 41, 71, 92
ACCESS open

Martorell, Bohigas, Mackay, Puigdomènech 1985–92

Martorell, Bohigas, Mackay, Puigdomènech 1985–92

Hotel Arts

The Olympic Village and Port masterplan by Martorell, Bohigas, Mackay featured two skyscrapers, then Spain's tallest buildings. They act as 44-storey beacons for the area, marking the entrance to the Olympic Port and standing out against a city backdrop of mostly low- and medium-height buildings. These markers straddle the Carrer de la Marina as it cuts through almost the entire city, from the Collserola hills via the Sagrada Familia and the monumental bullring until it reaches the seafront. Before this, the street came to a dead end in the RENFE railway yards. Each tower follows the same volumetric guidelines, a 33-metre x 33-metre plan and 153 metres high. Fraternal twins, they were commissioned from different architects who were left to decide upon the expression of each building.

Bruce Graham of the Chicago firm Skidmore, Owings, and Merrill was responsible for the tower that houses the luxurious Hotel Arts with 456 rooms and some private apartments on the upper floors. At the base of the hotel, lower-height buildings form a spa and shopping centre with underground parking. Frank Gehry collaborated with his latticed Fish sculpture that marks the precinct (see page 4.22). The architects have expressed the building structure on its exterior: a framework of white steel exterior trusses is gridded to a height of four storeys each. This vertical reading contrasts with the horizontal banding of stainless steel and glass of the neighbouring Mapfre office building by the architects Enrique León and Iñigo Ortiz of Madrid.

ADDRESS Carrer de la Marina, 19–21
CLIENT The Travelstead Group
METRO L4 Ciutadella/Vil.la Olímpica BUS 10, 36, 45, 59
ACCESS open

Skidmore, Owings, and Merrill 1992

Skidmore, Owings, and Merrill 1992

Fish

For years, fish have been a personal obsession for Frank Gehry, the Canadian-born, California-based architect most recently lauded for the extraordinary Guggenheim Museum in Bilbao. This enormous 35-metre x 54-metre copper-coloured steel-latticed fish marks the commercial and leisure complex at the base of the Hotel Arts tower (see page 4.20) in the Olympic Port.

As forms, fish express Gehry's strong connection to sculpture. Even his buildings are generated from non-traditional volumes and collisions. On a personal level, fish emerged from Gehry's childhood memories of the carp that swam around in his Polish-born grandmother's bathtub on Fridays, awaiting their fate as part of Saturday's Sabbath dinner. Perhaps they are also a tongue-in-cheek critique of the academic post-modernism and post-structuralism that were prevalent when the deconstruction of his own suburban LA house brought him to the attention of his peers in 1980. In this seaside context, the signature fish finds a suitably maritime location.

ADDRESS Passeig Marítim de la Barceloneta/Carrer de la Marina
METRO L4 Ciutadella/Vil·la Olímpica
BUS 10, 36, 45, 59,
ACCESS open

Frank O Gehry 1992

Frank O Gehry 1992

Meteorological Centre

Alvaro Siza of Oporto, the most important Portuguese architect of his generation, has carved into the simple cylindrical purity of this form to respond to the pressures of the site, creating a complex internal system of both centripetal and centrifugal forces within a void. Set along the coast, just at the edge of the Olympic port, the centre registers atmospheric conditions and changes in Mediterranean light levels. The exterior's two-part division of a concrete base and marble top actually corresponds to six levels behind. Vertical openings mark deep incisions that form indented light courts. The interior divisions have been created by radial walls and concentric screens. Around the 33-metre-diameter outer edge, monitoring operations are carried out. Spaces for weather prediction and communication are centred about a 9-metre-diameter interior court. Stairs are oriented between outer and inner cores. The cylinder opens directly to the sky. On the upper level an open stair leads to rooftop radar equipment and seaside views.

The lower levels of the cylinder have been cut away in response to the demands of the seaside promenade. The chamfers straddle an inclined plane and allow continuity of pedestrian and vehicular routes. A visitors' information centre is located in the partially sunken lower level and entered by a ramp.

ADDRESS Moll de Gregal, Carrer de l'Arquitecte Sert 1
METRO L4 Ciutadella/Vil·le la Olímpica
BUS 36, 42, 71, 92, 100
ACCESS visitors' centre only

Alvaro Siza 1989–92

Alvaro Siza 1989–92

Pergolas on Avinguda d'Icària

Each neighbourhood of Barcelona has its own model giants representing all human life from kings and queens to fishmongers and butchers. These literally larger-than-life figures are paraded through the streets on festival days. Enric Miralles and Carme Pinós have created these metal tree trunks with wooden lath foliage to evoke a procession of giants in the centre of the Avinguda d'Icària, the main interior street of the Olympic village. Real plantings were not possible because of the rerouting of the city's storm water run-off system

This dynamic parade addresses the new constructions lining the street. The wooden slats show how these architects rework a common local element, the pergola, in a fresh and unexpected way, somewhere between building and sculpture. As in earlier projects such as their plaza and pergola in Parets de Valls, the architects dramatise features related to the body, use and movement. The metal trees sway and bend with the wind as the tilted wooden plane hovers above.

ADDRESS Avinguda d'Icària
METRO L4 Ciutadella/Vil·le la Olímpica
BUS 14, 41, 71, 92
ACCESS open

Enric Miralles and Carme Pinós 1990–92

Enric Miralles and Carme Pinós 1990–92

Parc Poblenou

The young architects who won the competition for this seafront park, the largest along the coast, and for the Marbella Sports Pavilion and athletic track within it, already had reputations in landscape design. Both had worked in the studio of Elíes Torres and José A Martínez Lapeña, as well as having formed part of the municipal architecture team organised by Oriol Bohigas to execute his programme of parks and plazas in the 1980s.

Their intervention extends the adjacent operations carried out in the Olympic Village and Port. Rerouting Spain's first railway, a coastal line to Mataro which blocked off this industrial sector from the sea, opened 4 kilometres of beach to the city. Along this stretch the architects created a seafront park on the site of old industrial buildings, bordered by the working-class district of Poble Nou.

Parc Poblenou is treated as a series of layered, thin spatial zones, extending out from the urban grid to the sea. The layers move from the landscaped borders of the coastal highway on to sand dunes and sea grasses, low coastal pines, playing fields, playgrounds, beachfront cafés, open space for festivals, to boardwalks. These landscapes have been allowed to develop over time. They are watered by elevated sprinkler masts that simulate rainfall and reduce the salinity of sea air. Lighting marks different paths and itineraries.

The designers used the rusted, cut-up remains of the *Ashraf II* to create sculptures and the sense of a sea disaster. The boat had been immobilised on charges of smuggling for years before they decided to make use of it.

ADDRESS Ronda del Litoral/Avinguda del Litoral/Carrer de Carmen Amaya, Carrer de Llacuna
METRO L4 Poblenou BUS 36, 41, 92
ACCESS open

Manuel Ruisánchez and Xavier Vendrell 1988–92

Manuel Ruisánchez and Xavier Vendrell 1988–92

Marbella Sports Pavilion

This sports pavilion and its outdoor playing field are sited near to the beach within Parc Poblenou by the same architects (see page 4.28). The building's geometry and tectonic treatment contrasts with their work in landscape design. Originally built to house Olympic badminton and then to serve as a neighbourhood resource, the building was overrun with hundreds of cats because the period of transference proved to be protracted. The pavilion exemplifies the problems that occurred when projects designed for the Olympics were later handed over to local administrations: in some cases the theoretical plans did not coincide with actual local needs or means.

The building, with a capacity for 1000 spectators, is an abstract and minimal rectangular volume, with a 2.5-metre-high band of transparent glass at ground-floor level. The main playing floor was sunken, so as not to obstruct views to the sea. A cut-out patio on the northern side of the site offers access to what was meant to become a local library, exhibition gallery and the Poblenou archives.

The Olympics offered the city's architects ample opportunity to explore wide-span structures and to interpret typologies related to sports facilities. Here, 50-metre-wide steel trusses are supported on precast-concrete piers. The end elevations are faced with wood panels. The other two façades have tilted panels of Corten steel above a band of glass. The athletics field is covered by stone rubble and has been built into the site.

ADDRESS Parc Esportiu de la Marbella, Ronda del Litoral
METRO L4 Llacuna or Poblenou
BUS 6, 36, 92
ACCESS open

Manuel Ruisánchez and Xavier Vendrell 1988–92

Ciutadella

Manuel Ruisánchez and Xavier Vendrell 1988–92

Centre Civic Can Felipa

The industrial area of Poblenou, once known as the 'Manchester of Catalunya', may soon become the 'Silicon Valley of Catalunya' depending on the success of the city hall's initiative to attract high-tech industries and R&D companies to the area. The neighbourhood has been renamed 22@BCN; in reference to its district number and the internet start-ups that it seeks. The work carried out by Mateo on the former Catex factory predates this initiative and is one of the few industrial buildings that has been transformed into a public amenity. Much of the area's industrial heritage was demolished to make way for Olympic projects and housing developments.

The community and municipal sports centre was transformed over a series of years by Mateo during the same time that he served as editor of *Quaderns*. From 1981 to 1991, Mateo made the journal of the Col·legi d'Arquitectes de Catalunya a presence in international architecture debates by widening its thematic base and making it the first trilingual (Catalan-English-Spanish) architectural publication in Spain. Since then he has combined teaching at ETH Zürich with projects here and abroad.

Here the architect found a beautiful and vast structure of Catalan vaults supported on cast-iron columns with a mansard roof formed of fine wooden beams. Conceived of as a palace by its builders, the transformation of the ruined building respected that reading. Its reuse as a gymnasium required the addition of a new volume for a ground-floor swimming pool as well as consolidation of the overall structure.

Mateo composed the addition and interior spaces by adding a series of elements to contrast with the existing nave. Inside, natural light dematerialises the skins of lightweight, almost provisional materials. Service zones, showers and dressing rooms placed in the existing building are made of ephemeral partitions, granting spatial continuity to the original

Josep Lluís Mateo 1984–89

Ciutadella

Josep Lluís Mateo 1984–89

4.34

vaulted roof. The addition accommodates elements that were incompatible with the structure and dimensions of the existing building. A semi-exterior public bar has been juxtaposed with the nave. The swimming area has a concrete structure with glazed enclosures, a copper roof, and corrugated-metal sheeting.

Contrasting colours were used boldly to personalise each floor of the community centre which contains a small theatre, an exhibition space and a lecture hall under the roof. A vertical communication tower was built outside the nave and connected by glass-covered bridges. The solid tower lightens towards to the sky. At the highest point, a great glass surface is next to a metal plaque of digitalised information that looks a bit like a credit card. It shows the time and interestingly employs the raised dots of the Braille alphabet. Mateo also constructed the bordering block of low-cost housing.

Ciutadella

ADDRESS Carrer de Pallars, 277
METRO L4 Poblenou
BUS 40, 42, 92
ACCESS open

Josep Lluís Mateo 1984–89

Ciutadella

Josep Lluís Mateo 1984–89

Montjuic

Museu Nacional d'Art de Catalunya

The Olympic projects on Montjuic encompassed both sports facilities and cultural institutions, confirming the mountain as the city's largest urban park and as a repository of its most ancient and recent history: human remains dating back 10,000 years were discovered here. The name Montjuic is thought to refer to 'Mon Jovis', after the Roman dedication to Jove, or 'Mountain of the Jews' after an eleventh-century Jewish cemetery. The quarries which provided the stone for the buildings of the Eixample later became the site of mass executions during the civil war.

The National Palace was built in just 28 months by Pere Domènech for the 1929 World Exposition, which urbanised the hill with the new cosmopolitan *noucentisme* style of a generation of architects, some of whom had been trained under the modernist masters Lluís Domènech i Montaner and Gaudí. It closes the monumental axis leading from Josep Maria Jujol's neo-baroque fountain in Plaza Espanya, past Carles Buigas' Magic Fountain to the summit. This axial terraced plan was created in 1915 by Josep Puig i Cadafalch – who was excluded from participating in the 1929 exposition presented during the dictatorship of Prim de Rivera – for an Electrical Exposition that was never held. The parks were designed by the French engineer Jean C N Forestier with Nicolás M Rubió Tudurí and the roads were laid out by Josep Amargós. The Beaux-Arts architecture of the palace contains the largest covered hall in Barcelona.

The renovation coincided with an institutional mandate for a National Catalan Museum ratified in 1990. The Italian architect Gae Aulenti, known for her controversial transformation of the nineteenth-century Gare d'Orsay in Paris (1980–86) into an art museum, converted the building to house the national collection, including the exceptional examples of tenth-century Romanesque frescoes removed from remote churches in the Pyrenees. Part of the museum programme was to recreate

Gae Aulenti with Enric Steegman 1987–95

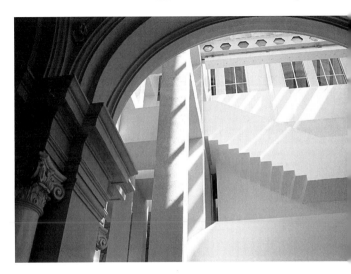

Montjuic

Gae Aulenti with Enric Steegman 1987–95

Museu Nacional d'Art de Catalunya

the spaces of the churches within the halls of the palace. During the civil war the gothic collection, in safekeeping away from Barcelona, was exhibited in the 1937 World Exhibition in Paris a few blocks away from Picasso's *Guernica*, as a symbol of Spain's endangered heritage.

In the reconversion of the palace, the architects dealt first with the difficult ascent which caused the isolation of this visually prominent building. Along the monumental axis escalators and terraces were added as well as landscaped lateral entries. The main façade was opened up with large surfaces of glass. The main romanesque and gothic galleries were situated on either side of the grand central hallway with separate entrances. Each is entered through a light court with glass-covered passageways. Other parts of the collection, temporary exhibition spaces and support services were located at a lower level where the architectural elements were restored and enhanced.

Aulenti handled the reconversion with a lighter touch than in the Gare d'Orsay. In fact against the original her interventions seem fragile and undersized. A stepping white metal structure was inserted along the edges of the great domed hall to accommodate the bookstore and cafeteria. (Antoni Tàpies wanted to hang a giant sock from the dome.) This intervention seems provisional in relation to the grandiose empty space that visitors have to cross to enter the tiny restaurant squeezed in at the back.

ADDRESS Palau Nacional Parc de Montjuic
METRO L1, L4 Espanya
BUS 9, 13, 30, 38, 56, 57, 157
ACCESS open Tuesday to Saturday, 10.00–19.00; Sunday, 10.00–14.30

Gae Aulenti with Enric Steegman 1987–95

Gae Aulenti with Enric Steegman 1987–95

Mies van der Rohe Pavilion

Built as the Weimar Republic's reception pavilion for the 1929 Universal Exhibition, this structure is widely recognised as one of Mies' most innovative buildings and the climax of his early career. From March 1930 when it was completely dismantled it existed only on paper and in photographs. The first proposal to rebuild the pavilion was initiated in 1953 by Oriol Bohigas, a member of Grup R. The idea was sanctioned by Mies but had no funding. The decision of the newly democratic city government in 1979 to reconstruct the pavilion was based on the desire to restore part of the city's history. It coincided with the creation of a new documentation and exhibition centre, the Mies van der Rohe Foundation, which awards prizes for European and Latin American architecture and represents Spain in DOCOMOMO, the international organisation for the conservation of architecture of the modern movement.

One of the landmarks of modern architecture, Mies' experimentation stood in marked contrast to the historicising styles around it. The raised podium and regular grid of eight cruciform chromed-steel columns make classical allusions with traditional materials while the centrifugal spatial arrangement of freestanding stone walls and glass planes forms a suprematist composition of horizontal spatial fluidity and transparency between interior and exterior. Subtle shifts in surface colour and texture, such as the use of transparent, green, grey and sand-blasted glass, against onyx, travertine, marble and water created mirroring, distortions and displacements. The space opens out to a reflecting pool on the podium and closes into a courtyard, pool and sculpture marked off by green marble from the Alps and dark glass. Mies and Lilly Reich designed a neo-Shinkleresque cantilevered metal chair especially for the occasion.

The investigation carried out on site and in Mies' archives in MOMA, New York, found that the pavilion's siting had not been neutral as was

Cristian Cirici, Fernando Ramos, Ignasi de Solà-Morales 1981–86

Montjuïc

Cristian Cirici, Fernando Ramos, Ignasi de Solà-Morales 1981–86

Mies van der Rohe Pavilion

previously assumed. Mies had rejected one site along the main axis, choosing the setting at the western end of the terraced concourse level, perpendicular to it. Bordered by rows of Ionic columns, Puig i Cadafalchs' Victoria Eugenia Palace provided a blank backdrop and profuse vegetation offered pedestrian paths and a natural edge at the back. Variations were made over the course of construction due to time and budget constraints. In the reconstruction, modern building technologies were applied to assure the building's permanence against the elements. A concrete roof slab replaced the original steel-beam structure.

The search for onyx slabs of adequate scale for the central wall involved real detective work. The original onyx that Mies bought from a Hamburg distributor had been cut to decorate the interiors of a transatlantic liner and had long since disappeared. The team made enquiries at quarries around the world until finally narrowing the search down to North Africa, from Egypt to Morocco. Eventually the large slabs were cut in an Algerian quarry that had long been closed down.

ADDRESS Avinguda Marquès de Comillas
METRO L1, L3 Espanya
BUS 9, 38, 65, 91
ACCESS open daily, 9.00–20.00

Cristian Cirici, Fernando Ramos, Ignasi de Solà-Morales 1981–86

Cristian Cirici, Fernando Ramos, Ignasi de Solà-Morales 1981–86

Montjuïc

Fundació 'La Caixa'

Set on the edge of Montjuic, the former Casaramona textile factory, built in 1911 by Josep Puig i Cadafalch, is one of the most impressive examples of modernist industrial architecture in the city. It will form part of a major cultural centre and the main exhibition spaces for the foundation, superceding their centre in the Casa Macaya on Passeig de San Juan, also by Puig i Cadafalch. Co-founder of the conservative Catalanist party, the Lliga Regionalista, Puig had been Catalunya's pre-eminent archaeologist. Here he referred back to the middle ages while addressing a twentieth-century development, building concept and scale. After 1920 when the factory closed down, a police station occupied the deteriorating complex.

Transformation involved the restoration of the three parallel wings of diaphanous floors with steel structure and transverse Catalan vaulting. A subterranean addition doubles the surface area to 12,000 square metres and is entered from a minimalist glass prism set within a sunken patio along Marquès de Comillas. Adjacent to the transparent vestibule cube are the stores, a mediathèque, library and an auditorium as well as art-storage areas. The original entrance has been displaced to connect the centre with Montjuic. To restore the ground floor, 41,712 bricks replicating the originals were used, 13 kilometres of micro-footings, and 3.5 kilometres of invisible beams. The cafeteria occupies one of the wings and exploits the original interior streets. New multi-use spaces will occupy the prominent corner towers, which once held water tanks. The centre opened briefly in June 2000 before construction resumed with the most-visited exhibition ever held in Catalunya: the centennial of the Barça football club.

ADDRESS Avinguda Marquès de Comillas
METRO L1, L3 Espanya BUS 9, 38, 65, 91
ACCESS opening scheduled for 2001

Roberto Luna, Francisco Javier Asarta, Robert Brufau 1998–2001

Montjuïc

Roberto Luna, Francisco Javier Asarta, Robert Brufau 1998–2001

The Olympic Ring

The 1992 Olympics fell into Barcelona's tradition of using world show-case events to urbanise areas of the city. The competition-winning scheme for the masterplan was awarded in 1984 to the same team who collaborated on the Olympic stadium renovation. Their plan followed the historical precedent of Puig i Cadafalch's design with a second monumental axis on the upper part of the mountain, along the Avinguda de l'Estadi where the 1929 neo-classical stadium by Pere Domènech closes the axis and acts as the primary focal point.

The monumental axis of the Olympic Ring follows the slopes dominated by the stadium. A terraced esplanade descends over three main levels, connecting the major buildings, commissioned from various architects. A series of 18-metre-high tubular glass lanterns recalls the style of the 1929 World's Exhibition and unifies the terraced levels as they are transformed into plazas, fountains, water courses, lawns and cascades.

The Palau San Jordi by Arata Isozaki is entered from the first level across a central lawn, bordered by a waterfall and stairway. Calatrava's Telefonica Tower is positioned off the second terrace with access to the Olympic pool remodeled by Moises Gallego and Frank Fernandez. The central round lawn and reflecting pool of the third level leads to the INEFC (the National Institute of Physical Education of Catalunya) training and education centre by Ricardo Bofill with a stair down to the baseball field below. The Sot del Migdia park was designed by Beth Galí.

ADDRESS Avinguda de l'Estadi, Passeig de Minici Natal
METRO L1, L3 Espanya
BUS 13, 61
ACCESS open

C Buxadé, F Correa, J Margarit, A Milá 1985–92

C Buxadé, F Correa, J Margarit, A Milá 1985–92

Olympic Stadium Renovation

This once-dilapidated structure hosted the symbolic opening and closing ceremonies of the Olympic Games. The renovation involved the conservation and restoration of the neo-classical masonry façade while the level of the field was lowered 11 metres to increase the stadium's capacity to 60,000. Vittorio Gregotti and his team added a 150-metre-long white metal canopy that follows the curve of the stadium seating while projecting out some 30 metres. It is tied by cables to a horizontal metal truss. The ambulatory encircling the stadium was widened on its upper end to provide spectator access.

Sculptures from 1929 restored and placed in their original positions include Pau Gargallo's *Charioteers* and *Olympic Horsemen*, set in front of the Porta de Marató and the main façade. The support for the Olympic flame was designed by the Catalan industrial designer André Ricard.

ADDRESS Avinguda de l'Estadi, Passeig de Minici Natal
METRO L1, L3 Espanya
BUS 13, 61
ACCESS open

V Gregotti with C Buxadé, F Correa, J Margarit, A Milá 1986–90

Montjuic

V Gregotti with C Buxadé, F Correa, J Margarit, A Milá 1986–90

Palau San Jordi

Isozaki's competition-winning design for an arena with a capacity of 17,000 people and a smaller multipurpose pavilion was built for the Olympic track events but now accommodates sports events, ice shows, congresses and concerts. The architect considered the project, with its eight-year duration, as a cultural exchange. He based the design of the sports stadium on a desire to use the most advanced technology while relating to the site and local traditions.

His initial models showed softly undulated roofs over both the arena and the pavilion behind. A series of parallel curving beams set along the axis of the main entrance suggested a new topographical surface and meshed with the base. Unfortunately this design was changed and the rectangular pavilion behind was built with a flat metal roof. The three-dimensionally curving roofs were constructed as a white space frame set on top of a very distinct plinth.

Instrumental technology was applied to solve the problem of a double-curved space frame. The 'pantadome' system invented by Dr Marnorp Kwaguchi introduced a constructive system where interlinking components were assembled on the ground. When raised into position by hydraulic cranes, the structural parts were connected and consolidated. This system avoided the extensive use of scaffolding normally employed for erecting this type of roof.

The zones of the stadium plan – the arena, seating and ambulatory – correspond to the three-part articulation of the covering: the space frame's dome and perimeter and a low sinuous zinc roof supported on yellow beams that act as a skirting between roof and plinth. While referring to Japanese architectural forms, the roof surface was covered with traditional ceramic tiles like those used in church cupolas. Skylights accentuate the edges. The roof sits as a separated entity on top of a traver-

Arata Isozaki and Associates 1983–90

Arata Isozaki and Associates 1983–90

Palau San Jordi

tine, brick and concrete plinth that adapts to the slope. The entrance portico is a concrete grid opening on to the esplanade where 36 concrete columns anchor flowing dynamic steel wires that whip the air. This sculpture which leads to the entry is by the Japanese artist Aiko Miyawaki and is entitled *Change*.

ADDRESS Avinguda de L'Estadi, Passeig Minici Natal
METRO L1, L3 Espanya
BUS 13, 61
ACCESS with admission to events

Arata Isozaki and Associates 1983–90

Arata Isozaki and Associates 1983–90

Telefonica Tower

This telecommunications tower is also a giant sundial: the mast is set to the same angle as the Earth's axis. As a giant urban sculpture, in its metropolitan scale and presence it may be contrasted with Norman Foster's tower on the crest of the Collserolla, built in the same period. Whereas Foster's tower has no pedestal and is tied by cables on to a natural hilltop setting, this sleek white steel element thrust upwards 120 metres from a grand circular base, covered with broken tile mosaics in homage to Gaudí. Anchored on the second plaza of the Olympic esplanade, it originally caused controversy because of its enormous scale and prominent setting.

ADDRESS Avinguda de L'Estadi, Passeig Minici Natal
METRO L1, L3 Espanya
BUS 13, 61
ACCESS open

Santiago Calatrava 1991

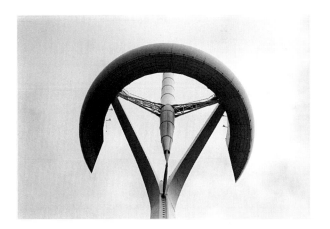

Montjuic

Santiago Calatrava 1991

Museu d'Arqueologia de Catalunya

Since 1935, the city's archaeological museum has been housed in a hexagonal building with wings that was built as the Graphic Arts Pavilion for the 1929 International Exhibition held on Montjuic. Designed by Raimon Duran Reynals, the structure is representative of *noucentisme*, the predominant style of the 1920s which signified a return to classical and Mediterranean references.

The renovation by Josep Llínas – also responsible for the renovation of Josep Maria Jujol's fanciful Metropol Theatre in Tarragona – sought to recover the museum's original spatial and constructive state, and refers back to the central hexagonal hall as the main distributor of the building. Llínas added a new floor, placing the public exhibition spaces above and leaving the ground floor for services. The wooden ceilings and light sources of the original building were retrieved and are highlighted against white walls and wooden display cases, stairs and flooring. The reconstruction of a courtyard in the wing along the entry axis was planned for the open-air exhibition of some archaeological elements. The mezzanine level makes better use of the central nucleus. A smaller hexagon was inscribed within it to create an exterior ambulatory for exhibition display. A new wooden roof was added within the central tower over the hexagon, which brings diffuse natural light into the space.

ADDRESS Passeig de Santa Madrona, 39–41
METRO L1, L3 Espanya
BUS 55
ACCESS open Tuesday to Saturday, 9.30–13.30, 15.30–19.00;
Sunday, 9.30–14.00

Josep Llínas 1984–89

Montjuïc

Josep Llínas 1984–89

Mercat de les Flors Municipal Theatre

The idea for the creation of the 'City of Theatre' started with this structure, formerly the city's central flower market. This experimental theatre is part of a concentration of theatre groups, performance spaces and dramatic arts schools, that involved refurbishing existing buildings and the construction of a new theatre institute.

The idea arose when the city searched for an appropriate place to present the experimental director Peter Brooks' *Carmen* in 1983. It ended up being performed here, in the grounds of the Agricultural Palace, a complex that remained from the 1929 International Exhibition. In 1985 the new space, a flexible experimental theatre without a fixed stage, was formally inaugurated with the work *Le Mahabarar*, also directed by Brooks. The building has two volumes and stages foreign and local productions. The empty unadorned shell of the nave serves as the performance space and the great domed vestibule with loggia houses the entrance, ticket office and bar. The cupola was decorated by the Mallorcan painter Miguel Barceló, who used to live in Barcelona.

The Palace of Agriculture will become the new home of the Teatre Lliure group. Gracia Fabià Puigserver and Manuel Nuñez Yanowsky will rehabilitate two wings into a flexible stage for 750 spectators. The third wing will house the administration and management, a bar, restaurant, a boutique and a second theatre in the form of a Greek cross.

ADDRESS Carrer de Lleida, 59
METRO L1, L3 Espanya or L3 Poble Sec
BUS 55, 38, 57, 61, N-0
ACCESS lobby open

Fontela i Mir 1985

Montjuïc

Fontela i Mir 1985

Institut de Teatre

This new building, along with the Palace of Agriculture and the Mercat de les Flors, forms part of the 'City of Theatre' complex, which also includes the Grec outdoor amphitheatre across the street and a sports palace located off site.

The Institute of Theatre created in 1913 is a centre for the dramatic arts. This new headquarters building is adjacent to the Mercat de les Flors municipal theatre (see page 5.24). The competition-winning project deals with a complex brief in a compact and seemingly effortless way, taking full advantage of the site's changes in level to provide mountain views and natural light. The main entrance faces an outdoor space shared with the other theatres. It has a glass façade with two side stone façades, and is covered by a metal-slat awning.

The building, a long tall bar with two lower wings, is actually various buildings that have been seamlessly joined. The structure houses two educational entities: the School of Dramatic Arts and the School of Dance and Choreography. Besides the 15,700 square metres dedicated to classes, studios and workshops, the building includes an auditorium, museum and two performance spaces. An Italian theatre with seating for 350 is located in the wing just beyond the Mercat de les Flors. The other is a workshop theatre space of 150 square metres. Additional elements include administration space, a bar and restaurant, parking, an archive and library of books, manuscripts and material related to the history of Catalan theatre.

ADDRESS Carrer de Lleida, 59
METRO L1, L3 Espanya or L3 Poble Sec
BUS 55, 38, 57, 61, N-0
ACCESS some spaces open

Ramon Sanabria and Lluís Comeron 2000

Montjuïc

Ramon Sanabria and Lluís Comeron 2000

Fundació Joan Miró Addition

In the Olympic period the Joan Miró Foundation's expanding activities necessitated the construction of an addition. This was carried out by Jaume Freixa, who had worked closely with Josep Lluís Sert on the original building. The extension closed off one of the courtyards to the right of the entrance and – in collaboration with the municipal government – created a new sculpture garden around the building.

The original building, designed from Sert's office in Cambridge, Massachusetts, where he served as dean of Harvard's architecture school, highlighted Miró's donated artworks by instigating routes around courtyard spaces. Sert was especially sensitive to the enriching possibilities of the relationship between architecture, painting and sculpture. This interest stemmed from his experience of building the Spanish Pavilion for the Republican government in Paris in 1937 where Picasso's *Guernica*, Julio Gonzalez' *Montserrat*, Calder's *Mercury Fountain* and Miro's lost mural *The Catalan Reaper* formed part of the exhibit. From 1939 onwards, during his years in exile in New York, Sert connected with the artistic and intellectual European émigré community. Through his involvement in CIAM (the International Congress of Modern Architecture, founded in 1928 and in existence until 1956), he wrote a theoretical text encouraging collaboration between architects and artists. In 1955 his friendship with Miró led to his first project in Spain since the civil war, the artist's own studio in Mallorca which, like the foundation, was a modern version of traditional architecture. The large workspace also allowed for a change in scale in Miró's work of the time.

The Miró Foundation also drew on Sert's experiences for the Foundation Maeght in San Paul de Vence (1959–64), in establishing relationships between the glazed interior with gardens, courtyards and terraces for the display of art. Mediterranean vernacular forms and the Catalan

Jaume Freixa 1988

Fundació Joan Miró Addition

Montjuic

Jaume Freixa 1988

vault were reinterpreted in rough concrete. Skylights projecting from the roofs with small barrel vaults allowed filtered light to enter, while creating a village-like atmosphere on the terrace above.

The foundation is set in wooded grounds with spectacular views. It promotes contemporary artists whose work is represented in the surrounding sculpture garden, including Tom Carr's *Needle* (1990) and Jaume Plensa's *Dell'arte* (1990).

ADDRESS Plaça de Neptú
METRO L1, L3 Espanya or funicular from Parallel
BUS 61
ACCESS open October to June: Tuesday to Saturday, 10.00–19.00 (except Thursday, 10.00–21.30); Sunday, 10.00–14.30. July to September: Tuesday to Saturday, 10.00–20.00

Jaume Freixa 1988

Montjuïc

Jaume Freixa 1988

Botanical Garden

A team of botanists, landscape designers and architects has transformed this former hillside garbage dump into a fractal and folding landscape. The land has been sculpted into an irregular geometric mesh of planted triangulated surfaces. The garden has been modelled and moulded by taking cues from the site's topography, unlike other interventions that have imposed themselves on the mountain. Covering more than 15 hectares, it is one of the city's largest green spaces.

From the visitors' orientation area, cut into the landscape with concrete slabs, a series of primary and secondary routes lead up, past a mosaic of plantings of Mediterranean species, grouped according to their ecological affiliations and local microclimates. Species from the Canary Islands, north Africa, Catalunya and the eastern and meridian Mediterranean fill out the central zone, followed by countries with similar climactic conditions such as Chile, South Africa, and coastal Australia around the edges.

The organisation of botanical ecosystems converged with the morphological idea of laying a triangular mesh over the terrain that can adapt itself to the specificities of different plantings. With slight movements to the heights of the vertices, the mesh fractures and facets, making each orientation and slope slightly different and unraveling at the edges. The facets have been constructed with double triangular concave and convex walls varying in height, length and radius. This fractal order allows the infrastructural networks, drainage and watering systems to be hidden. Triangular rest areas with seating introduce each zone with the most representative species.

The garden was designed for scientific and educational purposes. In the future an education centre will be built on an upper plateau. The architect has designed routes, signs and symbols and taken advantage of the

Carles Ferrater, Josep Lluís Canosa, Beth Figueras 1999

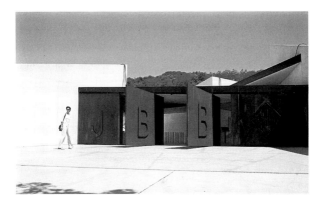

Carles Ferrater, Josep Lluís Canosa, Beth Figueras 1999

Botanical Garden

beautiful views. On the level of detail, the concrete sidewalk has been treated with different aggregates depending upon the slope. Watering is carried out by a state-of-the-art system using radio signals from metal masts, connected to a complex computer system with indications for each type of plant depending on the season. The route ends by passing two century-old olive trees from Morocco which have never been separated, and a reflecting pool to the exit.

ADDRESS Carrer Doctor Font i Quer, 1
METRO L1, L3 Espanya
BUS 50, 61
ACCESS open daily, 10.00–15.00

Carles Ferrater, Josep Lluís Canosa, Beth Figueras 1999

Carles Ferrater, Josep Lluís Canosa, Beth Figueras 1999

Fossar de la Pedrera

The first public administration elected after the transition to democracy took great care in restoring monuments that held special significance in Catalan culture, many of which had been removed or damaged during the Franco years. Sculptures were returned to their original sites and new works were dedicated to paying homage to collective memory. This communal grave in Montjuic was used to bury the victims of political executions carried out in the Montjuic Castle in 1939 and 1940, just at the end of the Spanish civil war. It was one of the first sites to be commemorated after the restoration of democracy.

The tomb of the Catalan president Lluís Companys, executed here in 1940, is set at the highest point of this landscaped site which is treated with a minimum of architectural elements. The grave is found after an ascent along a winding path that reaches a cypress grove. Stone plaques carved with the names of the victims of Franco's troops in 1939 form a solemn field. The sheer and rugged wall of the stone quarry which drops into a reflecting pool serves as a backdrop to a green esplanade. From here a pergola of concrete and steel leads to Companys' grave.

ADDRESS Carrer de la Mare de Déu del Port
BUS 9, 38, 72, 109
ACCESS open

Elisabeth Galí and Màrius Quintana 1983–86

Elisabeth Galí and Màrius Quintana 1983–86

Espanya

Barcelona Plaza Hotel

Although the team of Jordi Garcés and Enric Sòria is most associated with public institutional works and rationalist minimal architecture, here they have designed a commercial project for a 338-room hotel. Set in Plaça Espanya, this mid-rise perimeter block building with a small tower responds to its context. The tower relates to the development plan by the same architects for Carrer de Tarragona, an arterial road which ends in the plaza. Now designated as a new zone of tertiary activities and widened to 60 metres it is dotted by a series of high-rise office buildings. The hotel also relates to the convexity of the Arenas bullring and the concavity of Plaça Espanya itself. The site's irregular shape has been rationalised around a 30-metre-wide courtyard, following the typology used in grand old hotels such as the Ritz. The interior façade has been textured with ceramic tiles in five tones. Like Gaudí's light wells for Casa Batlló, the darkest colours are at the top where most light enters. Public spaces – reception, bars, and restaurants – are located on the ground floor. Convention facilities are underground with parking beneath. The tower accommodates eight suites and emerges from the tower block to mark the end of a roof-top swimming pool.

The outer façades form a taut skin of prefabricated panels of grey and red granite. The metal window mullions add to the pattern already found in the stone to form a tense graphic surface overall. The central clock recalls the one that existed on the site's original hotel, built in 1929 for the World Exhibition by Rubió Tudurí and later demolished.

ADDRESS Plaça de Espanya, 8
METRO L1, L3 Espanya
BUS 9, 27, 50, 56, 61, 109
ACCESS open

Jordi Garcés and Enric Sòria 1990–93

Jordi Garcés and Enric Sòria 1990–93

Parc de Joan Miró

Joan Miró was asked to lend his celestial imagination to this urban park, the first public plaza to be commissioned by the newly democratic city hall. The artist, then 90 years old, decided on the siting for this, his last and largest public work, a 22-metre-high concrete and ceramic sculpture entitled *Woman and Bird*. This work of art for Barcelona referred to his private lexicon of signs and ciphers, deeply connected to the logic of constellations. Even during his years in Paris with the Surrealists, Miró considered himself an 'International Catalan' and referred back to native influences: the Catalan Romanesque paintings now in the national museum, the mystic writings of the medieval philosopher Ramon Llull and the *trencadis* of Gaudí and Jujol's bench at Park Güell.

The park is set at the boundary of the Eixample and the industrial Sants neighbourhood, which became part of Barcelona in 1894. Miró's work rests in a reflecting pool in what was the first phase of the park: a hard plaza used for neighbourhood festivals, especially the traditional summer-solstice bonfires on San Joan's day. It is an erotic work: the woman is actually formed of a phallic shape cut open to reveal a long black incision. A bird that looks like a crescent moon adorns her hat. The broken tile work was carried out by the ceramists Joan Gardy Artigas.

Most of the site was covered by a grove of Mediterranean pines and palms in a later phase. The north-west quadrant is raised slightly above street level while the remaining area is sunken and reached by a pergola.

ADDRESS Carrer de Tarragona/Carrer d'Aragó/Carrer de Vilamarí
METRO L3 Tarragona, L1 Espanya
BUS 27, 30, 38, 65, 109
ACCESS open

Joan Miró and A Solanas, A Arriola, B Galí, M Quintana 1980–82, 1985

Espanya

Joan Miró and A Solanas, A Arriola, B Galí, M Quintana 1980–82,

Plaça del Països Catalans

This exploration of light-transparent elements set against a backdrop of urban chaos was one of the first projects of the 1980s public plaza programme. It exemplifies many projects that followed: the regeneration of Barcelona has favoured enigmatic landscapes and new topographies rather than spectacular singular buildings, in contrast to Bilbao, whose urban transformation is based around Frank Gehry's Guggenheim. This refined minimalist work became one of the city's most internationally recognised new architectural works.

On an undefined space in front of the Sants railway station a series of ephemeral gestures reinterprets such traditional outdoor elements as the pergola, canopy, market shed and fountain to create an artificial terrain. Plantings were not possible and only lightweight structures could be supported over the subterranean train tunnels just below the surface. The architects used this situation as an opportunity for exploration and created a focal point more visual and symbolic than actually occupied.

A series of elements is unified by an abstract ground plane of granite paving. A low linear pergola with an undulating roof points in the direction of the station. A 15-metre-square canopy structure supported on thin steel poles with metal mesh roofing is complemented by a serpentine line of wooden benches, a row of metal fountains, a clock, tables for chess and the silhouette of a cat. Lighting theatrically changes the landscape at night.

ADDRESS Sants railway station
METRO L3, L5 Sants-Estació
BUS 27, 30, 43, 109, 544
ACCESS open

Viaplana and Piñon with Enric Miralles 1981–83

Viaplana and Piñon with Enric Miralles 1981–83

Tecla Sala Cultural Centre

L'Hospitalet de Llobregat, an independent municipality to the south of Barcelona, is developing a series of urban-regeneration programmes along its train lines, including a major hotel and office complex by the Richard Rogers Partnership. Tecla Sala, an existing exhibition space within a former textile factory, had to share a 94-metre x 28-metre nave of three floors with a new central library for the town. The programme required that the surface area be divided in two. The intermediate level had to be shared equally, favouring the creation of a multipurpose room there. A centralised entrance for both was created on this floor which holds part of the library.

Albert Viaplana devised an entry ramp that acts as a prolongation of the street, from one end of the site to the common entry hall. A stairway with a double-height space leads to the main part of the library above. A vestibule to the exhibition hall leads to an interior double ramp down to the existing hypostyle hall of steel structural elements with Catalan vaults below.

A public garden has been created by using the project's most singular exterior element: the ramp with crisscrossing routes which organise the entire landscaped space. As in other reconversion projects by these architects, a preference for oblique angles, views and passages, and for insertions and juxtapositions of elemental boldness highlight and mark out the differences between the old and new.

ADDRESS Carrer de Josep Tarradelles, 44, L'Hospitalet de Llobregat
METRO L1 Torrassa
ACCESS open Tuesday to Saturday, 11.00–14.00, 17.00–20.00; Sunday, 11.00–14.00

Albert Viaplana 2000

Espanya

Albert Viaplana 2000

Glòries

Plaça de les Glòries Catalanes

On paper, Plaça de les Glòries had always been a new centre of the city. In the 1859 Eixample plan by the engineer Cerdá, the plaza appeared as an important symbolic element: the confluence of the major road axis into and out of the city, the meeting point of the Meridiana, the Diagonal and the Gran Via. Leon Jaussely's 1911 scheme of annexed towns created an embellished urban centre, complete with library, post office and markets. In reality, however, the plaza was the largest and most centrally located urban void in the city.

The plaza remained an unfinished residual site. The surrounding neighbourhoods had become run down. Railway lines ran through it. The plaza acted as an obstacle to the continuity of the road network: the Meridiana never reached the Ciutadella Park, the Diagonal didn't end at the sea. It was transformed as part of one of the infrastructural projects carried out in co-ordination with Olympic Barcelona. The aim was to create more than just a road junction and with the current continuation of the Diagonal to the sea, Plaça de les Glòries does indeed mark a new geographic centre of an extended Barcelona.

On a technical level, the railway lines were buried, freeing up the space and allowing the extension of the road system. The storm sewer was rerouted to pass to the sea. An elliptical ring with two levels was created, a green space defined in its centre. The upper level connects Gran Via with the seafront ring road and the lower level allows the Meridiana and the Diagonal to continue to their respective ends. The structure contains parking for 800 cars.

To upgrade the neighbourhoods, a series of new cultural institutions was commissioned to border the plaza. These include the National Theatre of Catalunya by Ricardo Bofill and the Music Auditorium by Rafael Moneo. The Farinera Cultural Centre was created in a factory

Andreu Arriola 1991–92

Andreu Arriola 1991–92

building at the edge of the Meridiana, which has been transformed into a more pedestrian-friendly street. The Parc del Clot and the North Station Park and sports centre are nearby.

In a later phase of completion an outer ring for local traffic will increase the circumference of the plaza, creating an intermediate green zone that has been designated for the siting of new cultural institutions, including Zaha Hadid's proposal for a 'City of Cinema'. From there, the Diagonal's continuation to the sea will be dominated by a series of controversial high-rise object buildings marking the Poble Nou district now named 22@ and starting with Jean Nouvel's 21 storey Agbar Tower. The glass phallus is meant to recall some of Gaudí's grouped peak-like towers but in singular form.

ADDRESS Plaça de les Glòries Catalanes
METRO L1 Glòries
BUS 7, 56, 60
ACCESS open

Andreu Arriola 1991–92

Andreu Arriola 1991–92

Auditori de Barcelona

Although born in Navarra and educated in Madrid, Rafael Moneo influenced a generation of Barcelona's architects when he taught in the architecture school from 1970 to 1980. He then went on to develop a more international profile as Director of Harvard Graduate School of Architecture where he holds the honorary Sert chair. In the 1980s he received two highly visible commissions in Barcelona: the publicly financed Auditorium and the private L'Illa shopping centre, a 'horizontal skyscraper' on the Diagonal. These works coincided with a moment in his career marked by major commissions for emblematic cultural buildings in other parts of Spain, such as the Pilar and Joan Miró Foundation in Palma de Mallorca and the Kursaal Center in San Sebastian.

The Auditorium building was commissioned for this site to invigorate the neighbourhoods around the Plaça de les Glòries. Begun during the Olympic period, work proceeded slowly as funding became scarce. Although inaugurated after more than ten years of construction, the building is still awaiting the completion of a second hall. Built as the home of the Barcelona City Orchestra, Moneo described his building as a project forced into its own contained and compacted autonomy in relation to the characterless and uninspiring surroundings. The building's horizontal volume occupies a long site on the Eixample and responds to a change in the tone of the street network as the Meridiana enters the grid. The building's façade faces the axis of Ausiàs Marc Street and bridges its extension.

Two volumes – each one containing a concert hall, one with seating for 2500 and the other for 700 – are connected by a plaza that is both covered and voided. The foyer between the two halls is in fact a covered public square: a pedestrian entry with a 'lantern impluvium', an illuminated glass void at its heart. This space, which is open to the sky, is used

Rafael Moneo 1988–98

Rafael Moneo 1988–98

Auditori de Barcelona

to mark distances and define contiguities. To avoid a reading of two separate buildings, shared dressing rooms and services at the upper storey and basement levels connect the complex and varied programme which includes rehearsal rooms, a music museum, a library with separate entrances, the Institute for Advanced Music Studies, a recording studio and experimental music room, and a restaurant.

The work offers a dialectic between a tough urban exterior and a refined interior, expressed in its materials. The gridded reinforced-concrete exterior is infilled with Corten steel panels. The interior of the main auditorium is a faceted rectangular abstract space veneered in warm oak.

ADDRESS Carrer de Lepant, 150
METRO L1 Glòries
BUS 7, 56, 62, N-0, N2
ACCESS public spaces open; access to interiors with admission to concerts

Rafael Moneo 1988–98

Rafael Moneo 1988–98

Teatre Nacional de Catalunya

Both the airport addition and the National Theatre represent a third phase in Bofill's work, which combines curtain walls and hi-tech detailing with classical concrete columns and elements. These buildings mark a change from the studio's earlier work found in the architect's own home and office in the converted silos of a concrete factory, or the Walden, the seven-apartment building beside it in San Just Desvern. The latter recalled the forms of Archigram, but was covered with ceramic tiles, and proposed a vertical social organisation on open exterior streets. These projects brought the Taller international recognition in the 1970s.

Large-scale French housing projects in the 1980s marked a second phase of experimentation with social-housing minimum standards. Their monumental neo-classical forms were fabricated of refined precast concrete panels. They made Bofill the only exponent of scenographic post-modern historicism in Spain. Some of the Parisian satellite town projects became sets for Terry Gilliam's vision of post-apocalyptic totalitarianism in the film *Brazil*.

The theatre was commissioned in 1987 by the Catalan regional government, who defended the building's monumentality when it was inaugurated some ten years later. Set beside Moneo's auditorium, a structure of similar size, the two relate less to the site than to their own internal organisation. The new cultural buildings are like ships docked at the Plaça de les Glòries, destined to become a new centre for greater Barcelona.

Conceived of as a glass temple, Bofill's structure houses a 1000-seat repertory theatre, a 400-seat experimental theatre, a theatre school and a grand rehearsal space. A scenery workshop is located behind in an independent bar. A grand gesture has been made with the giant, glazed palm-tree lined lobby, which leads to the repertory theatre enclosed by a

Ricardo Bofill – Taller de Arquitectura

Ricardo Bofill – Taller de Arquitectura

Teatre Nacional de Catalunya

concrete amphitheatre wall. It is a great gathering space with pavilions for ticket sales and cloakroom, a bar, and a restaurant located on the amphitheatre roof. The plaza in front of the temple's stairs was planned as an external performance space.

ADDRESS Plaça de les Arts, 1/Carrer de Padilla/Carrer de Castillejos
METRO L1 Glòries
BUS 7, 56, 62, N-0, N2
ACCESS open

Ricardo Bofill – Taller de Arquitectura

Ricardo Bofill – Taller de Arquitectura

Parc Estació del Nord

This immense park takes advantage of the buried railway tracks of the now converted North Station. The former railway terminal (Andrés i Puigdoler, 1861) has been tranformed into a central bus station, police station and sports facility where the Olympic table-tennis competitions were held. A new tunnel for the rail lines was only partially submerged along the building façade and is hidden by an inclined plane of paving and stairs. The park is formed of 17,000 square metres of freed-up land and will expand to 22,000 square metres after expropriations from surrounding constructions.

The park has been conceived of as an earthwork that both camouflages and incorporates the train tunnel. The scale of the ceramic sculpture mounds by North-American artist Beverly Pepper was integral to its conception. *Trencadís*, the traditional broken ceramic work mostly associated with Gaudí, has been used at a monumental scale to create three thematic zones. Six hundred square metres of tile work were carried out by Catalan artisan Joan Reventos. *Fallen Sky* is a low *trencadís* hill surrounded by grass. *Spiral of Trees* is formed by radial plantings. A third element, a ceramic wall, appears from the ground like a giant wave. Urban furnishings such as the Corten steel poles were designed by Pepper.

This park was planned at the same time as the Archive of the Corona d'Aragon by Lluís Doménech and Roser Amadó to provide the neighbourhood with institutions of cultural importance.

ADDRESS Carrer de Napoles/Carrer Amogàvers/Carrer de la Marina
METRO L1 Arc de Triomf
BUS 40, 42, 54, 141
ACCESS open

Beverly Pepper with A Arriola, C Fiol, and E Pericas 1985–91

Beverly Pepper with A Arriola, C Fiol, and E Pericas 1985–91

La Farinera de Clot

In recent years the city administration has facilitated the reuse of several historic buildings as community centres. In Clot, the new centre is housed in a 1900s flour factory. Training in new technologies is on offer, in response to the new realities facing residents of this traditionally working-class area.

Designed with a modernist aesthetic by Josep Pericàs in 1898, the four-storey, rectangular brick building of cast-iron structure and Catalan vaults was covered with ceramic decoration and sloped roofs with Arabic tiles. Originally, the floors were divided by a wall perpendicular to the main façade – wheat was cleaned on one side and flour was produced on the other. The original structure has been restored, preserving the vertical wooden conduit system that fed flour to the different machines and mill.

Three new volumes facing the Plaça de las Glòries play off the original structure. Transparent glass marks the points of intersection between the old building, a Corten steel cylinder and a concrete stair and ramp tower. The ground floor, which houses an exhibition space, internet café and a museum, has a single-storey reception addition with wood lath screening the façade. The basement level is dedicated to communication technologies, with television- and radio-editing rooms. The first floor is used for workshops and meeting rooms for neighbourhood organisations. Social-services offices are on the second floor and on the uppermost floors there is an auditorium for 180 people.

ADDRESS Gran Via de les Corts Catalanes, 837/Carrer dels Escultors Claperós
METRO L1 Glòries, L2 Clot
BUS 56, 60, 62, 92
ACCESS open

Carles Sanfeliu and Josie Abascal Rovira 1999

Carles Sanfeliu and Josie Abascal Rovira 1999

Parc del Clot

This neighbourhood park occupying the grounds of the old RENFE railway station and workshop was created at the same time as other public parks laid out on former industrial sites, including the Parc de l'Espanya Industrial on an abandoned factory in Sants, and the Parc de la Creuta del Coll in an old stone quarry. These places were represented to their working-class neighbourhoods as new recreational and symbolic focal points. Community involvement helped to determine their form. The Parc del Clot addressed the lack of public services and community spaces in this dense area of San Martí de Provencals.

On the 3-hectare triangular site, the architects created a landscape of changing ambience and artificial topographies where walkways and paths, zones of rest and play overlap and crisscross. The remains of the original brick walls now enclose *The Rites of Spring,* a bronze angel by North-American artist Bryan Hunt. A ruined wall of arches is transformed into an aqueduct fountain of cascading curtains of water. The designers created a sunken zone of playing fields, contrasted with a series of planted areas. Earth excavated from the playing fields was used to create mounds and hills. Glass towers are sculptures by day and lighting at night.

Two elevated walkways connect the most travelled routes through the site, linking the district headquarters to the market and marking a path from a smokestack to the Clot Farinera. The park creates a central focus for the undefined perimeter edges of the bordering buildings.

ADDRESS Carrer dels Escultors Claperós
METRO L1 Glòries or Clot
BUS 56, 60
ACCESS open

Daniel Freixes, Vicente Miranda and Victor Argenti 1984–87

Daniel Freixes, Vicente Miranda and Victor Argenti 1984–87

Bac de Roda Bridge

This project, commissioned by the Barcelona City Hall, anticipated the current regeneration of the Sagrera area and the knitting back together of two large areas of the city divided by the main train lines. As Barcelona awaits the arrival of the high-speed train line linking the city to Madrid and Paris, plans are underway to bury the tracks and create a linear park here, bordered by new housing. The pedestrian and vehicular bridge by Santiago Calatrava, the Valencian-born engineer and architect based in Zürich, marks the beginning of this new zone of intervention. The support arches elevated over the roadway suggest a flight trajectory. This urban stitch is a landmark, an object stretched over a void and a sculpture all at once.

The bridge spans 140 metres and connects the streets Felipe II and Bac de Roda with the Eixample grid. Twin steel parabolic arches span the tracks. Each set of arches forms a single complex entity, where the outer arches incline inwards to brace the interior arches. Connecting top and centre, they broaden out beyond to allow the passage of the sidewalk. The road deck and sidewalk are suspended on four lines of cables which enclose the pedestrian zones to form a hybrid urban space: lookout, street, and plaza in equal parts. Four stairways follow the lines of the arches and will lead to the planned station and park. The bridge is grounded via a concrete abutment and night lighting has been incorporated into the design.

The bridge is adjacent to a small urban space created during the same period as part of the city's urban regeneration policy. Designed by Olga Tarrassó of Barcelona's urbanism and municipal services department, the Plaça General Moagas is punctuated by two sculptures by Ellsworth Kelly. Bordered by the streets Felipe II, Palència and Sagrera, just where Calatrava's bridge enters the street grid, Tarrassó divided the site into two

Santiago Calatrava 1985–87

Bac de Roda Bridge

Glòries

Santiago Calatrava 1985–87

7.22

triangular zones: one planted and outlined by brick, and the other of earth marked by a 20-metre-high concrete monolith and a triangular fold of Corten steel.

During the Olympic period Tarrassó developed the continuous beach-front and port-side promenades in the Barceloneta neighbourhood.

ADDRESS Carrer de Felipe II/Carrer de Bac de Roda
METRO L5 Navas
BUS 33, 34, 35, 43, 71, 544
ACCESS open

Glòries

Santiago Calatrava 1985–87

Glòries

Santiago Calatrava 1985–87

Plaça de la Palmera

This plaza forms part of the network of urban foci and public spaces created in the early 1980s during the initial phase of urban regeneration that brought Barcelona to international attention. Under the guidance of Oriol Bohigas as head of municipal planning, these projects were delimited, small-scale interventions that sought to remedy and enrich the impoverished conditions of Barcelona's outer suburbs, rapidly built up during the Franco era in response to mass immigration from the rest of Spain. They were known as 'projects without plans' because they followed a piecemeal approach, offering a short-term attempt to create neighbourhood spaces and a 'monumentalisation of the periphery'.

The North-American artist Richard Serra, known for testing the boundaries between sculpture and architecture, was invited to create *The Wall* in an empty lot. The only existing element was a palm tree. As the art critic Rosalind Krauss wrote in *Sculpture in the Extended Field*, Serra's work may be defined by negation: not strictly architecture, sculpture or landscape, it overturns and crosses traditional categories. His austere intervention gives form and meaning to the new space. The two concrete concentric walls that divide the plaza mark off two distinct metaphorical landscapes: a rich, green zone of trees and a bandstand lined by cobblestones, and a barren, sand-covered desert used by children as a playing field, where two acacias stand alone.

ADDRESS Carrer d'Andrade/Carrer de Maresme/Carrer del Concili de Trento
METRO L4 Besós, La Pau
BUS 42, 56, 60
ACCESS open

Richard Serra 1981–83

Richard Serra 1981–83

Parc Güell

Parc Güell Restoration

In the 1980s some of Gaudí's projects became UNESCO World Heritage sites. Casa Milà, Palau Güell and Parc Güell all underwent years of restoration. The goal here was to repair and consolidate the structure and decoration of this most emblematic work: to return it to its original appearance by replacing damaged elements with identical pieces of greater quality. The restoration focused especially on areas where Gaudí had tried out innovations such as prefabrication. It was carried out by a team of architects with a special affinity for the modernist master and Josep Maria Jujol, his collaborator.

Parc Güell was in reality a failed real-estate project, designed as an anthology park, with thematic follies and stylised landscape treatments and architecural elements. The industrialist Eusebi Güell had planned to follow Ebenezer Howard's Garden City model on Pelada mountain, just as he had looked to English models for his enlightened factory town, Colonia Güell. He was involved in railroads, banking and textiles and held the Spanish patent for Portland cement, which was used in the prefabricated parts of the park. Gaudí lived in the only model house built of the 60 shown in the masterplan. He constructed a topography of viaducts and roadways so that residents could go from their homes to the market hall with its grand plaza above.

This central element was in the worst state of disrepair. The classical columns of the market hall of 100 columns (only 88 were built) were an allusion to a Roman road that once crossed the site and were fabricated of artificial cast-stone pieces. The small domes, laid side by side to form the ceiling, were prefabricated out of a combination of ceramic bricks and cement, covered with artful *trencadis* (broken tiles) collages by Josep Maria Jujol. Hollow tubes in the centre of the columns allowed the collection of much-needed rainwater in an underground cistern. An undulating

Elíes Torres and José A Martínez Lapeña 1986–90

Elíes Torres and José A Martínez Lapeña 1986–90

bench, both parapet and seating, delimits the plaza above.

Restoration work had previously been done on the bench and *trencadis* and the load of the roof had been lightened by emptying it of rubble fill, especially in the areas of double spans where columns had not been placed. The rest of roof was badly damaged by leakage from the clogged drainage system. The lintels between columns had deteriorated and needed to be replaced without dismantling the domes. New water-proofing was added and the plaza was refilled with a light aggregate, lessening the load and improving the insulation.

The restoration of the decorative *trencadis* by Jujol required investigation. The tile work revealed a secret mystical religious text. During the restoration, the ingenious system of metallic porticoes invented by Gaudí to support the prefabricated cement bench was discovered. Many ceramic pieces were missing and scale photographs of each section were taken in order to have the irregular forms of tile precisely remade. Many capping tiles had fallen off or been replaced without care. The outer part of the bench was tiled with the signs of the horoscope and stylised architectural elements recalling acroteria. Inside, a hidden cryptic ode to the Virgin was scrolled across its length. Sometimes incised, scratched or written upside down were phrases such as: 'Son Front' (her forehead), 'En tu la vida' (Life in you), or the Virgin's symbols, the rose and crown.

ADDRESS Carrer d'Olot, Avinguda de Coll de Portell, Carretera del Carmel
CLIENT Ministerio de Cultura and Barcelona City Hall
METRO L3 Vallcarca
BUS 24, 25
ACCESS open

Elíes Torres and José A Martínez Lapeña 1986–90

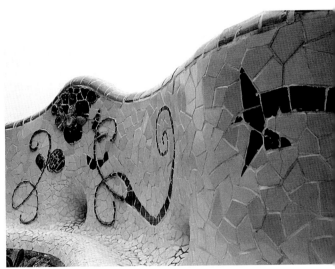

Elíes Torres and José A Martínez Lapeña 1986–90

Parc de la Creueta del Coll

The steep stone walls of this former quarry in the Collserolla hills are a dramatic setting for a public park and gathering area commissioned when Oriol Bohigas was head of urban planning. The central organising element of the southern area of the park is a circular tracing – sometimes an earthen plaza and sometimes a swimming pool – with a central concrete island of palm trees. *Totem (1987)*, a rusted steel sculpture by the American artist Ellsworth Kelly, marks the end of the entrance ramp. The circle has been inscribed in its setting by terraces whose steps form amphitheatre seating. The northern wooded area of the park contains playing fields and recreational areas.

The Basque sculptor Eduardo Chillida created the main symbolic focus of the park. He had already been commissioned by the city hall to create a public art piece when he visited the quarry. He insisted on choosing his own site: a dramatic curving cliff of stone at one end of the park. His *Eulogy to Water* refers to the myth of Narcissus. An enormous 80-ton block of concrete with tentacle-like forms was cast on site. The suspended form is completed by its reflection in a laminate of water, separated out from the swimming pool and surrounded by the natural backdrop.

Chillida began exploring the sculptural possibilities of concrete in the 1970s; although normally associated with sculptural bases, the surprise and beauty of Chillida's piece is that it goes against this assumption. The concrete mass is held in place by four cables. It is a poetic study of mirroring, lightness and weight, tension and stasis.

ADDRESS Avinguda de la Mare de Déu del Coll
METRO L3 Vallcara
BUS 25, 2
ACCESS open

Josep Martorell and David Mackay 1981–87

Parc Güell

Diagonal

Traffic Signals

Calatrava earned his degree in architecture in his native Valencia and trained in civil engineering at the ETH in Zürich, where his office is based. His sculptural designs for bridges and other infrastructural projects are animated by references to natural structures such as animal skeletons, to dynamic kinetic systems and to the concept of force. His influences range from Rodin and Brancusi to organic forms. Some of these sources may be seen in this public commission for the traffic signals along the Avinguda Diagonal, above the Plaça Francesc Macià where this major crossroads leads out of the city to the start of the motorway.

The architect has transformed these normally banal elements of the urban landscape into dynamic, seemingly animated lines. The lane signals have been integrated into a light tubular steel structure that seems to pull across the six lanes of roadway that they span. The tubes taper together at a central meeting point in the vertical supports at the street edge. These supports appear to be held in a tension rather than static.

The city's regeneration worked on all scales: from enormous infrastructural projects down to paving patterns, urban furnishings, lighting, kiosks and bus stops. This concern for small-scale elements that make up the urban landscape is also seen in the yellow roofed bus shelters around town, designed by Elíes Torres and Antonio Martíinez Lapeña, some of which have been replaced in recent years by a new design by Norman Foster.

ADDRESS Avinguda Diagonal beyond Plaça Fransesc Macià
METRO L3 Maria Cristina, Palau Reial or Zona Univeristat
BUS 6, 7, 33, 34, 63, 67, 68, 78
ACCESS open

Santiago Calatrava 1986

Santiago Calatrava 1986

L'Illa Diagonal

With a 300-metre-long continuous street façade and a hybrid programme, this building has been conceived as a 'horizontal skyscraper'. It occupies what had been the largest vacant lot along the Diagonal; a wide artery designated by the Cerdá plan that changes its character many times as it cuts through the Eixample and loses its compactness on the way out of the city. Much of the planning along the Diagonal's eastern end favoured freestanding buildings in contrast to the Eixample perimeter block. This development responds to both: somewhere between the enclosed block typology of the Cerdá plan and the open and discontinuous object-oriented planning of the 1960s and 1970s.

This long superblock, equal to three Eixample blocks, varies in height from seven to 14 storeys with three underground levels. Winner of an international design competition in 1986, it includes offices, an apartment hotel and a shopping centre. Behind, there is a park with an hotel, convention centre and schools. The architects were concerned with how to break down the mass of the long façade. They have created a sense of variation and different perspectives through facets and setbacks that add life and interest to the continuous grid of windows. Perforations in the dark-green stone base create public entrances and a sense of permeability to the double-height interior shopping mall, which has been treated as a longitudinal interior street with light metal trusses.

ADDRESS Avinguda Diagonal, 555–559
METRO L3 Maria Cristina
BUS 6, 7, 33, 34, 63, 66, 67, 68
ACCESS open

Rafael Moneo and Manuel de Solà-Morales 1986–93

Rafael Moneo and Manuel de Solà-Morales 1986–93

Hilton Hotel

This 290-room hotel is set perpendicular to the Diagonal. With two parallel bars, it forms an 'H' scheme. The architects thought of the hotel as a giant urban door joining two public spaces: one that already existed and one created according to zoning regulations.

A new entry court has been marked by a vertical metal canopy on tall slender steel columns. The granite cladding goes against the glass curtain walls typically used in this area of the Diagonal. The façades are treated as diptychs: they have been split in the middle, each side with different tones of stone around the horizontal windows and the recessed three-storey glass entrance.

ADDRESS Avinguda Diagonal, 589
METRO L3 Maria Cristina
BUS 6, 7, 33, 34, 66
ACCESS open

Viaplana and Piñón 1987–90

Viaplana and Piñón 1987–90

Aparthotel Atenea

Almost all of Mateo's buildings are found at the outlying edges of downtown Barcelona, in the periphery or the suburbs. In response to these types of urban conditions, he has said that he maps the space between limits, stressing atmospheric issues of instability, movement and fleeting expression versus stability, weight and rootedness.

This stark project for a relatively small mixed-use complex deals with such themes in a banal setting. Its elemental architectural forms comprise two slabs and a plinth with a parking ramp. Set off the Diagonal, this combination hotel, shopping centre, parking and office complex is bound to the beltway more than to traditional urbanism. The circular glass towers of the Trade Building by Coderch and Valls (1966) are framed from Mateo's raised plinth by two slabs of different height and length.

The slabs seem to slide in relation to each other. They contain a traditional hotel distribution of rooms; part of one slab is given over to offices. Façades are treated with different skins relating to the interior uses. The raised plinth is formed by the roof of the shopping centre acting as a connector between the slabs, with a conference centre and several floors of subterranean parking below. Curved sections over the reception area and restaurant are the only hints of luxury.

Above the plinth is a stark urban space marked by a chequerboard pattern that in the original scheme was shown as a graphic enlargement of drops of water, an analogy to this architect's desire to solidify the vaporous conditions of the urban edge.

ADDRESS Carrer de Joan Güell, 207–211
METRO L3 Maria Cristina or Les Corts
BUS 7, 33, 59, 63, 67, 68, 70, 72, 78
ACCESS open

Josep Lluís Mateo 1990–92

Josep Lluís Mateo 1990–92

Classroom Building, Facultat Dret

In 1950, a new university zone was planned on the Diagonal's western end; construction of the first building began in 1955. Part of the motivation for this 'out-of-town' campus location was control: it was not by chance that the university zone is divided by the six lanes of the Diagonal; on some curbsides it still reads 'Generalissimo Franco' Avenue. Built during this repressive era, the idea was to isolate rebellious students from the city centre, especially urgent in the case of politically active law students. A plan for the new faculty was written in just three months; the building was completed nine months later. Designed by Guillermo Giráldez Dávila, Pedro López Iñigo and Xavier Subías Fagés, the law school's rationalist international-style use of prefabricated elements went against the neo-classicism used in university buildings up until that time.

Llínas' new classroom building, conceived as a rural house set in the city, sits on a wooded slope and fractures itself over the site. The architect sought to establish a relationship with the natural setting rather than with the existing buildings or city. This justifies the use of materials that change over time: concrete walls and copper roofs (which follow a slope parallel with the ground). The building has been embedded into the terrain to achieve maximum surface area with minimum contextual impact. The 85-metre-long structure has been fragmented into three parts. The breaks mark out pedestrian routes between the two existing buildings. Sometimes the fragments align with the school, at other times with the street.

ADDRESS Avinguda Diagonal, 684, Avinguda de Pedralbes
METRO L3 Palau Reial
BUS 7, 33, 74, 63, 67, 68, 75, 78
ACCESS open

Josep Llínas 1993–96

Josep Llínas 1993–96

Jardins Villa Cecília

This city park project has been carried out by two architects with a special affinity for landscape, metaphor and intervention. The practice of Torres and Martínez Lapeña stands out in Barcelona for its varied modes of working. Elías Torres has taught landscape at the architecture school since 1979 and this team was in charge of the restoration of Parc Güell (see page 8.2), taking great care in replacing the *trencadis* of the famous bench by Josep Maria Jujol. The anecdotal, poetic and detailed work of this architect/painter, Gaudí's most talented disciple, serves as an important reference for these designers.

The grounds of the Quinta Amèlia, formerly a private estate, were to be added to an existing French-style city park across the street. The architects' handling of this addition is poetic, idiosyncratic and unexpected. Mediterranean plant species were added to unite the two grounds. The architects sculpted the topography, boundaries and terrain, inserting surrealistic elements into the garden. The entrance has been painted with a *trompe l'oeil* garden gate. Metal trees with enormous tropical leaves overhang a reflecting pool and are bordered by a tall cypress garden hedge. A bronze sculpture of the drowned *Ophelia* by Francisco López Hernández is face down in the water, set against a blue wall. Garden paths edged in white stone lead to a children's park with a playing field. A wall of metal leaves marks an exit.

ADDRESS Carrer Santa Amèlia, 29–33/Eduard Conde/Trinquet
METRO L3 Maria Cristina, FFCC Sarrià
BUS 6, 16, 34, 66, 70, 74
ACCESS open

Elíes Torres and José A Martínez Lapeña 1982–86

Hotel Juan Carlos I

The high-rise atrium hotel type developed by John Portman in Atlanta and in the Los Angeles Buenaventura Hotel has been revisited and transformed into a sculptural object of concrete screen walls and glass. Built during the Olympic period, the hotel is situated at the end of the Diagonal in a zone of low density, in the grounds of the former Torre Melina rural estate. Ferrater has made three interventions at the point where the Diagonal leaves town to meet up with the highway system: the hotel, its subterranean fitness centre, and a new conference centre facing the roadside.

Two great solid concrete walls fan out to reveal a faceted glass volume. These wedges define the hotel's exterior entry court and support the porte-cochère. Inside they are vertical installation towers that contain fire stairs, air-conditioning and extraction ducts, chimneys and other service installations. Fanning out from them to the south are two 14-storey wings with hotel rooms set around a faceted elliptical atrium of great height and elegance. Above, where the polygonal roofs overlap, natural light enters. The royal suite is set under the last roof. The first-floor level contains a vestibule, hotel reception area, travel and car-rental agencies, banks, and the hotel management. On the mezzanine level there is a business centre, fitness club and a restaurant with access to a garden above the car-entry point. A series of reception rooms off the garden fans out and can be opened up to accommodate 1200 people.

The interior spaces have been created by sliding the concrete armatures to form facets. The atrium space is articulated by two planes, the first a concrete cornice, and the second of glass with cast-aluminum handrails, set before the space leading to the individual suites. The atrium has been divided vertically into three parts: the first 10 metres (the technical floors) have curved inclined surfaces; the second responds to the treatment of

Carles Ferrater and Josep M Cartaña 1988–92

Carles Ferrater and Josep M Cartaña 1988–92

the 12 floors of rooms, and the last two floors have been set back. They contain the technical floor with the royal suite above.

In the lawn next to the hotel, a fitness centre has been cut into the ground. This berm building is formed of radiating concrete walls, where layers of grass are peeled back to reveal a central reflecting pool.

ADDRESS Avinguda Diagonal, 661–671
METRO L3 Zona Universitat
BUS 7, 33, 67, 68, 74, 75
ACCESS open

Diagonal

Carles Ferrater and Josep M Cartaña 1988–92

Carles Ferrater and Josep M Cartaña 1988–92

Palau de Congressos de Catalunya

Many recent projects by Carles Ferrater have played with the articulation of different parallel volumes that seem to shift in relation to each other. This new conference centre has been designed as three volumes of varying height and width, separated by interior streets that bring in natural lighting and allow for visual communication between the Diagonal and the gardens of the Melina estate. The sleek solid forms have been cut into with different types of apertures, horizontal bandings of windows and large openings.

The main volume houses the entrance and an auditorium for 2500 people, with a banquet hall and kitchens below. The central volume is subdivided into rooms of smaller sizes. Above is a versatile multipurpose room with moveable panels to accommodate exhibitions and product presentations. The cafeteria is set in the smallest, naturally lit, organically curving volume.

ADDRESS Avinguda Diagonal, 661–671
METRO L3 Zona Universitat
BUS 7, 33, 67, 68, 74, 75
ACCESS inauguration scheduled for 2001

Carles Ferrater and Josep M Cartaña 1996–2001

Diagonal

Carles Ferrater and Josep M Cartaña 1996–2001

Ronda d'Alt

Ronda d'Alt

Before the construction of Barcelona's ring road, traffic into and out of the city passed through the centre. In contrast to other traditions of planning where the roadway came first and urbanisation followed, in Barcelona many local areas had became built up and needed to be set into a greater metropolitan network. Opened in 1992, the beltway formed an essential urban armature, linking the four major Olympic sports areas of Montjuic, the Diagonal, Vall d'Hebron, and the Olympic port and village. The beltway mediates between local and regional flows, improving accessibility to the city's outlying areas. Responding to the varied conditions it passes, the beltway forms an anecdotal system of linked sequences covered with bridges, pedestrian walkways, public facilities and gardens.

By the time that Barcelona built its ring roads, beltways in many other cities had reached such levels of saturation that Los Angeles, for example, the model of a car-based city, was building a metro. Although it had appeared in the 1953 county plan as a simple segregated roadway and again in the 1976 metropolitan plan, the protests of neighbourhood groups who feared the impact of such a project on their areas succeeded in blocking construction. The project was revisited as the key infrastructural work of the Olympic period, but guided by a new set of criteria and design concepts in response to the involvement of grassroots groups, who had had a strong tradition dating back to the Franco era. They demanded that the beltway be sunken in some areas and covered by platforms, playing fields, plazas and areas for walking.

This delay worked to the benefit of the design. The various sections of the project are works of civil engineering steered by formal and architectural issues. In its response to movement and passage the ring road acts like a bracelet with the Olympic areas hanging off of it like charms. With

Josep Antonio Acebillo, Francesc Figueras 1990–92

Josep Antonio Acebillo, Francesc Figueras 1990–92

its connections to tunnels running through the Collserola range and to the regional highway system, it allows a wider metropolitan reading for Barcelona beyond its geographic limits of the mountain, sea, and rivers. The Collserola range becomes a giant regional park instead of a border.

Over some of its length, the roadway has been treated as a double trunk system formed of six sunken segregated high-speed lanes with lateral lanes for local traffic. Some of the most interesting treatments are along the sequence of the Ronda d'Alt, which links the Vall de Hebron area and tunnels to the other side of the mountain. Lateral roads are sometimes cantilevered over the segregated lanes in response to geographic conditions. Highlights include the public facilities on a slab at Nou Barris by Marcià Codinachs and Mercè Nadal, the public space and playing field over the Collserola interchange by Victor Rahola at Plaça Alfons Carles Comín and the Nus de la Trinitat where a park fills the void of the highway interchange.

The roadway also provided the opportunity to construct 26 kilometres of new service galleries along its border. Prefabricated reinforced-concrete-block channels contain cables for electricity, telephone, fibre optics, traffic signals and public lighting.

ADDRESS Ronda d'Alt
METRO L3 Vall d'Hebron or Montbau, L1 Trinitat Vella
BUS 17, 60, 73, 85
ACCESS open

Josep Antonio Acebillo, Francesc Figueras 1990–92

Josep Antonio Acebillo, Francesc Figueras 1990–92

Torre de Comunicació de Collserola

Visible from all over the city, this totem-like structure set on the Collserola mountain range became an immediate landmark of Olympic Barcelona and is still widely referred to by the name of its architect. An object of high technology, it makes a strong contrast to its natural setting. The Foster Tower was the competition-winning design for concentrating the communications installations once scattered over the mountain.

The designer was aware of the impact that this enormous new visual ingredient would have as a powerful reference point and linchpin of Barcelona's greater metropolitan area on both sides of the hill. For Foster, infrastructural elements are emblematic structures too important to be left to chance, given their visual presence and scale. The tower was designed with this in mind. Technical elements were placed outside, allowing for adaptation to new technological developments.

The tower makes use of tensile structural technologies more commonly associated with bridge building. Outside the slender reinforced-concrete nucleus hang 13 curved triangular metallic platforms. The 205.5-metre-high tower has no pedestal. It is anchored to the ground by pre-tensioned cables tied to the lowest platform level. Three ties connect the metal structure to the concrete shaft and the 85-metre mast rising from the top of the core. At the highest level is a panoramic lookout with views of the city and the Collserola mountain, designated as a park and protected area.

ADDRESS Turó de Vilana, Tibidabo
FUNICULAR de Vallvidrera to bus 211
BUS T2 to 211
ACCESS 'Mirador' observation deck open Wednesday to Friday,
11.00–2.30, 15.30–20.00; Saturday and Sunday, 11.00–20.00

Norman Foster & Partners 1989–92

Norman Foster & Partners 1989–92

Ronda d'Alt

Museu de la Ciència

Giant freestanding letters on a mound across the Ronda d'Alt announce the building's presence, but the first intervention in this historic building predates this team's renovation of the Picasso Museum. Here the architects transformed a modernist hospice built between 1904 and 1905 by Domench i Estapà to create an interactive science museum.

The architects reordered the interior, creating a new entrance and stair, with the aim of achieving clarity and spaciousness. The built volume has been partially substituted in the area of a mediocre 1940s addition to the original long bar building. This transparent central entry hall differentiates the original structure from the addition and leads to a terrace behind. Façades were reclad in brick. 'Click', an interactive area for young children, was designed by Alfredo Arribas, Miguel Morte and Javier Mariscal.

An immense thematic science park designed by Esteve and Robert Terrades will convert the original building and subsequent additions into a mere backdrop to a new complex extending from the Ronda to Carrer Quatre Camins. A 15,000-square-metre outdoor public science park will be set next to an new 1500 square-metre hall with a recreation of the Amazon jungle's microclimate below. The new centre will be transparent and diaphanous, meant to engage the passive consumer into the wonders of science. The science park will include a garden of Mediterranean species representing the biological sciences and observatories and sundials for the physical sciences. The internal area of the museum will increase from 6000 to 24,000 square metres.

ADDRESS Carrer Teodor Roviralta, 55/Císter, 64
TRAIN FFCC Tibidabo and Tramvia blau
BUS 17, 60, 73, 85
ACCESS open Tuesday to Sunday, 10.00–20.00

Jordi Garcés and Enric Sòria 1979–80 and 1989

Ronda d'Alt

Jordi Garcés and Enric Sòria 1979–80 and 1989

Velòdrom d'Horta

This area on the slopes of the Collserola range had suffered a series of developments since its fourteenth-century origins, when hermits chose the hill for their retreat from worldly concerns. Nothing remains today of the gothic monastery they built, which was destroyed by invading French troops in 1808. Traces of the idyllic rural setting and private houses of the nineteenth century may still be found in El Laberint, formerly a country estate but since 1970 a public park. The picturesque landscape was dramatically altered and finally disappeared in the 1960s when housing for 55,000 people was built with little connection to the centre of Barcelona.

This early 1980s' project for a cycle track brought a monumental element to the area, filling out one of the urban voids and acting as an initial gesture toward planning in this abandoned landscape. It is sited with direct relation to the access for the Parc del Laberint and surrounded by gardens with a sculpted itinerary by the visual poet Joan Brossa (see page 10.14). The relative isolation of the Velodrom ended with the subsequent construction of the Ronda d'Alt (see page 10.2), the upper ring road built to connect the Olympic areas. Although the structure predates these operations, it now forms part of the Vall d'Hebron Olympic Sports area set on the hill just below the Ronda.

The formally pure and elegant wooden cycle track has been partially built into the slope of the hill, and adds pubic space to the area. A climb up steps leads past olive trees and Brossa's visual poem to an outdoor public plaza where up to 4000 spectators congregate to be seated. A circular outer ring contains services and leaves open zones between the wall and the elongated oval form of the track and tiered seating inside. The wall is formed of alternating passages of solid brick and perforated piers, and its circular purity relates to the axis of the gardens outside. The

Esteve Bonell and Francesc Rius 1984

Esteve Bonell and Francesc Rius 1984

use of two levels exploits the sloping site: for the public the upper-level track with seating and ring wall; for the athletes and press a lower-level access. Built in only ten months with an economy of means, materials and geometries, the work exhibits a complexity that goes far beyond its constraints.

ADDRESS Passeig de la Vall d'Hebron
METRO L3 Montbau
BUS 27, 73, 76, 85
ACCESS open for events

Esteve Bonell and Francesc Rius 1984

Esteve Bonell and Francesc Rius 1984

Visual Poem

The architects of the cycle track (see page 10.10) were admirers of Joan Brossa, the Catalan artist and writer and a former member of the Dau al Set group which included Antoni Tàpies. Brossa's activities included art, theatre and performance as well as visual poetry. This work which deals with evolutionary process was incorporated into the park surrounding the Velodrom. It is a visual poem, a walkable itinerary in three parts: *Birth*, *Pathway with Pauses and Intonations*, and *Destruction*. A giant stone letter 'A' forms the garden gate. Question marks and other punctuation marks such as full stops and commas are spread out along the grass. The path leads finally to the letter 'A' in ruins, broken into crumbled pieces at the end of the route and surrounded by tortured olive trees, cypresses and weeping willows.

In 1995 Brossa also created a homage to Roman Barcelona, *Barcino*, set in the Avinguda de Catedral leading to the Carrer Bisbe which was the Roman *decumanus*.

ADDRESS Passeig de la Vall d'Hebron
METRO L3 Montbau
BUS 27, 73, 76, 85
ACCESS open

Joan Brossa 1984

Visual Poem

Ronda d'Alt

Joan Brossa 1984

Vall d'Hebron Olympic Area

Eduard Bru is director of Barcelona's school of architecture and a theorist of contemporary architecture as constituting a new form of landscape. He treated the design of this 37-hectare site on the lower slopes of the Collserola range as an exploration of non-traditional open space. This triangular precinct with an 80-metre change of level was designated as one of the 12 new Olympic centres and one of the four main sports areas. After the games the area became a local recreational facility in what was once a desolate, disconnected built-up area from the 1960s housing boom. For Bru the site was a residual urban void, a left-over space lacking definition. His aim here was to create a 'piece of city', a free space that was neither traditional street, plaza nor park.

His urban-design layout was organised as a series of terraced platforms serving as playing fields. At the uppermost level, closest to the ring road, the Ronda d'Alt, the 220-metre-long metro depot was an enormous accidental given. In the end, it became one of the plan generators, organising the modules of successive stepping levels. The platforms nearest to the road are sports pavilions. Their geometries contrast with the curving flow of streets that follows the natural riverbeds of the site. Together they form a patchwork of rectangular stepping surfaces alternating with triangular precincts.

The terraced platforms were defined in four major levels: above the Ronda d'Alt was the existing cycle track. Below it, Bru positioned the Vall d'Hebron Sports Pavilion, designed by Garcés and Sòria; the archery fields and training centre by Miralles and Pinós; the municipal tennis centre by Antoni Sunyer; the Nou Vall d'Hebron residential press village which became housing after the games, and a hotel designed by Carles Ferrater, Josep M Cartaña, Joan Josep Forcadell, Ferran Pla and Robert Suso. Beyond these, at the lowest level, lies the Clota Park with the recon-

Eduard Bru 1989–91

Eduard Bru 1989–91

structed Pavilion of the Spanish Republic and works of public sculpture by Claes Oldenberg and Susana Solana. In addition to the overall urban scheme and the refurbishing of the Saint Genis Metro Depot, Bru designed a swimming-pool complex fitted into the roadway at the lower end.

At the level of material and detail, Bru also questioned traditional urban paving, lighting and furniture. He chose to make a statement by using artificial and industrialised elements associated with highways, airports and sports fields. Red, green and yellow artificial lawn materials cover 8000 square metres of the terraced platforms. An esplanade is paved with cushioning rubber tiles made from recycled truck tyres and edged by concrete gutters. Vertical airport-lighting elements are scattered about the site, along with metal benches and railings. Pedestrian routes suggest highway overpasses with galvanised-metal roadway curb barriers.

ADDRESS Passeig de la Vall d'Hebron
METRO L3 Vall d'Hebron or Montbau
BUSES 27, 60, 76, 85
ACCESS open

Eduard Bru 1989–91

Eduard Bru 1989–91

Vall d'Hebron Sports Pavilion and Municipal Fronton Complex

This sports facility is monumental and minimal at once, characterised by its use of skylights to enhance the playing courts. Two spatially distinct sports installations, each with its own entrance, are contained within one low cubic brick volume, whose façades have been abstractly marked by the main entrances, as well as functional elements such as drainpipes, horizontal slits for ventilation ducts and emergency exits. The project anchors the first terraced platform level of the triangular Vall d'Hebron Olympic area, following the masterplan designed by Eduard Bru. The entrances face the upper ring road, with the building set at a slight angle to this infrastructural element.

Athletes enter the multi-purpose Sports Pavilion and the Municipal Fronton Complex, set to the other side of the container, from a lower level, while spectators enter from above. The Fronton Complex, with seating for 2900 spectators, has a monumental sky-lit passageway, which distributes visitors to the main court on one side and two smaller courts on the other. A strong horizontal reading is created by the tripartite division of walls: a band of transparent glass at the base allows views into the playing areas; a brick middle zone is about the same height as the white skylights volumes above. A series of geometrically tapering skylights illuminates the playing courts; almost hidden from view on the exterior, they emerge in corrugated metal cladding from the flat roof.

ADDRESS Passeig de Vall d'Hebron, 166–176
METRO L3 Vall d'Hebron or Montbau
BUSES 27, 60, 76, 85
ACCESS open

Jordi Garcés and Enric Sòria 1990–91

Vall d'Hebron Sports Pavilion and Municipal Fronton Complex

Jordi Garcés and Enric Sòria 1990–91

Archery Range and Training Centre

The architects took advantage of the minimal brief requirements as an opportunity to take formal and constructive experimentation to the maximum. The changing facilities and training installation for the archery field built for the Olympic Games were to be used for neighbourhood soccer and rugby afterwards. They are two separate structures on the second level of stepping platform terraces determined by Eduard Bru's masterplan for Vall d'Hebron (see page 10.16). Both structures are carved into the mountain and exploit the idea of the building as retaining wall, using the shifts and displacements of the moved earth to define the spaces. The structures form a new dynamic configuration somewhere between building, landscape and sculpture, characteristic of the work of this team, both in their early thirties at the time of the commission.

The first building is formed by the fluid varied spaces between the retaining wall and the skewed repetition of prefabricated elements that act as shower and changing rooms. These are laid out as a series of shifting concrete screens. The architects explored the possibilities of a retaining wall moulded to the different rhythms of the occupants. Translucent glass covers the space between the roof and the curved concrete elements. This irregularly shaped gap is the circulation zone between the repetitive shower units and the earth wall. A pergola of industrial metal gratings covers the access ramp which is entered from a zone of curving asphalt paving.

In the second building the disjunction of the roof planes, supported on concrete columns with the organic curving ceramic brick walls below, recalls a dynamic seismic occurrence: an earthquake or eruption. The retaining wall has been formed by gabions, wire mesh wrapping stone rubble. Now common in the work of other contemporary architects, Miralles and Pinós were among the first to experiment with the system,

Enric Miralles and Carme Pinós 1989–90

Enric Miralles and Carme Pinós 1989–90

usually used in river engineering. Gabions also appear in their cemetery project in Igualada (see page 13.2). The shape of the wall defines the project areas. Breaks between roof slabs are edged with U-shaped metal forms and allow light to penetrate the interior.

Miralles and Pinós have played off many diverse influences, synthesising them into their own sculptural language. From the local vernacular, Gaudí's more geological constructions such as the viaducts and the roads of Park Güell or the crypt of Colonia Güell are brought to mind, as are Coderch's organic Mediterranean walls. Some of the tilted planes recall constructivism; and from the Smithsons, with whom Miralles and Pinós studied, is the idea of the building as an itinerary related to movement at the scale of the individual user.

ADDRESS Carrer de les Basses d'Horta and Avinguda Martí-Codolar
METRO L3 Vall d'Hebron or Montbau
BUSES 27, 60, 76, 85
ACCESS open

Enric Miralles and Carme Pinós 1989–90

Enric Miralles and Carme Pinós 1989–90

Tell Me, Tell Me Dear

Two folded, bent, and curved sculptures of oxidised metal planes gesticulate and converse at the end of the axis of an inclined esplanade of rubber tiles. The work changes as the viewer walks around it. The artist from Barcelona is known for her conceptually driven abstract work and her experimentation with a wide range of materials and evocations. This piece has been constructed of four sheets of Corten steel with a concrete base.

ADDRESS Avinguda Marí i Codolar
METRO L3 Montbau or Vall d'Hebron
BUS 27, 45, 73, 76, 85
ACCESS open

Susana Solana 1986–92

Ronda d'Alt

Susana Solana 1986–92

Pavilion of the Spanish Republic

The reconstruction of this historic building, now used as a library, is symbolic, and commemorative. Coinciding with Olympic Barcelona, the rebuilding of Josep Lluís Sert and Lluís Lacasa's Pavilion of the Republic – originally commissioned for the Paris World Exposition in 1937 – sought to re-establish the ruptured connection and continuity with the modern movement in Barcelona. Unlike the contemporaneous recreation of Mies van der Rohe's 1929 German pavilion in its original place in Montjuic (see page 5.6), the Sert building had no direct relationship to this site.

The original pavilion was built a year after the civil war had begun. The socialist architect Sert had been leader of the Barcelona organisation of the modern movement, the GATPAC, the Spanish wing of CIAM. Their work was cut short when the civil war sent Sert into exile. In the 1930s he had invited Le Corbusier to Barcelona to create an urban design known as the Plan Macía. The GATPAC was involved in activities ranging from publishing a magazine to proposing a city of leisure for working-class people on the sea just beyond Barcelona, which included demountable, factory-produced summer cottages. (Among the few works built by members of the GATPAC are the seven-storey Casa Bloc communal dwelling with duplexes, daycare and swimming pool which was derived from Le Corbusier's 'redent' prototype for the Ville Contemporaine, Sert's Tuberculous Building in the Raval, and an apartment block on Carrer de Muntaner, 342–348.)

Sert's original World's Fair Pavilion in Paris stood a block away from the Vatican Pavilion which housed a mural of Santa Teresa crowning Franco's nationalists, by his uncle, Josep Maria Sert. The central focus of Sert's pavilion was Picasso's monumental commemoration of the dead of Guernica, the Basque village bombed on market day by Hitler's forces.

Miguel Espinet, Antoni Ubach and José Miguel Hernández 1992

Miguel Espinet, Antoni Ubach and José Miguel Hernández 1992

Pavilion of the Spanish Republic

In front of it in an outdoor space stood Alexander Calder's mercury fountain (now in the Fundació Miró) as well as Miró's 'Catalan reaper' mural, now lost. The original pavilion was dedicated to showing art in favour of the republic and a programme of photomontage and symbolic work by politically engaged artists.

The architects of the construction used what little information there was available to build a structure true to the spirit of the original. Using industrial materials, modifications included a basement level with services and the addition of an office block. The materials and colours capture the spirit of the original. *Guernica* was displayed on the wall of a great covered outdoor space in a courtyard with cloth awnings.

ADDRESS Carrer Jorge Manrique, Avinguda Cardenal Vidal i Barraquer
METRO L3 Montbau or Vall d'Hebron
BUS 27, 45, 73, 76, 85
ACCESS open

Miguel Espinet, Antoni Ubach and José Miguel Hernández 1992

Ronda d'Alt

Miguel Espinet, Antoni Ubach and José Miguel Hernández 1992

Matches

There are more than 500 outdoor sculptures in Barcelona, part of the policy of urban renewal. The works range from historic and commemorative ensembles to works by contemporary international and local figures. Some are related to the creation of new public spaces and others, such as *Match Cover* by the pop artist Claes Oldenberg, provide visual enhancement at the curve of one of the irregular sidewalks in the Vall d'Hebron Olympic area. Oldenberg is known for his giant scale sculptures of everyday objects, ranging from binoculars to ice-cream cones. The five *Matches* point upward and one is lit. They were made of painted steel and fibreglass on a concrete base.

ADDRESS Avinguda Cardenal Vidal i Barraquer
METRO L3 Montbau or Vall d'Hebron
BUS 27, 45, 73, 76, 85
ACCESS open

Claes Oldenberg 1992

Ronda d'Alt

Claes Oldenberg 1992

Via Júlia

Via Júlia, the 900-metre-long central axis of Nou Barris, is a case of urbanisation after the fact. This area grew up in the 1950s and 1960s, due to immigration from other regions of Spain. The working-class neighbourhoods that sprouted up while Porcioles served as Barcelona's mayor during the Franco era were characterised by speculation: mass housing without planning or amenities. Many members of the newly elected democratic city hall of 1979 had been involved with the neighbourhood associations which proliferated at the time and which had developed a tradition of participation and protest, so they sought to address their concerns. Under Oriol Bohigas, head of urban planning, many projects focused on regeneration, improving urban services and connections and providing new cultural symbols.

An unpaved mound marked the centre where the tunnel for metro construction was left visible to save costs, causing a marked difference in levels between the two lanes. This was remedied by applying two differentiated sections and creating a pergola in between. *The Favencia Tower* by Antoni Rosello marks the northern end of the avenue as a great beacon. *Júlia: Homage to the Immigrants* by Sergi Aguilar is placed where the street changes its section. In the centre of the Plaza de Llucmajor designed by Viaplana and Piñón, the *La Republica: Homage to Pi i Margall* (1932) was re-erected. This controversial tribute by Josep Viladomat (1899–1989) to the President of the First Republic was removed by the triumphant Franco regime three years after its unveiling on Passeig de Gràcia.

ADDRESS Via Júlia
METRO L4 Lluchmajor, Roquetes
BUS 11, 12, 31, 32, 47, 50, 51, 73, 76, 77
ACCESS open

Josep Maria Julià Capdevila/Bernardo de Sola Susperregui 1982–86

Ronda d'Alt

Josep Maria Julià Capdevila/Bernardo de Sola Susperregui 1982–

Park at Trinitat Road Junction

Nus de la Trinitat at the meeting point of Trinitat Vella and San Andreu marks the northern entrance to Barcelona. The sunken park and the roadway interchange that define its exterior form were conceived of together. They form one 'event' or linked passage along the general operation of the ring road (see page 10.2). Carried out with a strong sense of formal design, these are civil-engineering projects guided by architectural concerns. They sought to redefine the approach to the integral design of roadscapes, infrastructure, public space and topography. Josep Antonio Acebillo directed the general planning.

In its giant scale and conception this intervention is closely linked to earthworks and land art and creates a mark of entrance into the city visible from the car. Resolving the connections of the northern and eastern highways with the city's beltways, this project lessens the visual and acoustic impact on the neighbourhoods by enriching the normally interstitial, left over spaces with public amenities, planting and promenades.

The interchange and park, with its overall 15-metre drop with respect to the road, is located on the alluvial and bedrock deposits of the former meander of the Besós river and occupies the last open space in the area. It has been conceived of as a single project in its treatment of plants, hydraulics and topography, as well as public facilities and spaces. These elements follow the riverbed and are grouped in linear bands, forming continuous lines. Mediterranean plants cover a spherical hill emerging from the lowest elevation. The park includes tennis courts, a lake with rowing boats, and pathways.

ADDRESS Nus de la Trinitat
METRO L1 Trinitat Vella
ACCESS open

Enric Batlle and Joan Roig 1990–93

Ronda d'Alt

Enric Batlle and Joan Roig 1990–93

Badalona

Badalona Sports Palace

This enormous structure, for 12,000 spectators, was conceived by the architects – the authors of the pristine cycle track in Vall d'Hebron (see page 10.10) – as a sports 'cathedral' due to its inward-looking autonomy and its contextual rupture with the surrounding urban fabric. It has been handled as an object of refined articulation. Here the self-contained, elongated elliptical structure is sited in a dense urban setting at an angle to the local street pattern of Badalona, on the other side of Barcelona's Besòs river border. Characterised by restraint and lightness, it was built to house the Olympic basketball competition. Its vastness meant that structure and roof treatment were two of the essential themes of the project.

The main entrance cuts into one end of the ellipse, creating a strong directionality. The volume is treated with a lean, stripped elegance both modern and archaic. The saw-toothed roof of patinated corrugated steel is set on a base modulated with a tripartite articulation: a lower dark-green stone base with projecting stairs; a green stone middle section; and a white metal portico, supported on thin vertical props. The base chamfers out at the long end of the ellipse to reveal the main entrance stair.

Two tiers of seating have been partially excavated into the ground. Access is via an ambulatory that forms the main circulation. In the areas with services, it is low and supported by ellipsoidal concrete piers. The taller, wider part rises to the roof. Six enormous composite sheet-steel trusses form the roof structure with their immense scale and elemental boldness. These trusses have a double inverted pitch, with an arch cut out of the apex and a tension cord angled over the prop.

ADDRESS Carrer de Ponent, 143–161, Badalona
METRO L4 Gorg
ACCESS open for events

Esteve Bonell and Josep Maria Gil 1987–91

Esteve Bonell and Josep Maria Gil 1987–91

Gran Velvet

Almost all of Alfredo Arribas' work during the 1990s was dedicated to entertainment centres and located in Japan and Germany: a revolving restaurant on a tower, fun houses and theme parks. Set against the backdrop of Barcelona's municipal concern for the 'public good', critics severely attacked or disregarded some of Arribas' early work as frivolous, extravagant and excessive. Yet projects like Gran Velvet not only anticipate his later foreign projects but point to a new ludic trend for recreational containers and media spaces proliferating worldwide – from Japanese Pachinko parlours to Times Square in New York. Arribas has explored such globalised sites with remarkable results.

Gran Velvet is a macro discothèque, a strange highway rest stop: a machine for playing. Set on an isolated parking lot in Montigalá, an industrial and suburban area of Badalona, this is one of the few freestanding works by Arribas built in Barcelona. The project is a 4000-square-metre multispace container – with a club, a performance space, and a dance floor on three levels. It is thematically linked to Arribas' 1987 Barcelona bar Velvet, inspired by the film *Blue Velvet*.

A kidney-shaped emblem reminiscent of 1950s road architecture and lounge design marks the entrance from the parking lot to a covered porch. A streamlined concrete base is punctured above by two cylinders of different heights. The taller of the two reaches a height of 24 metres and is covered by metal mesh and lighting, acting as a nocturnal marker. In the interior it contains a mobile stage platform that moves up and down over the dance floor and can support the load of a swimming pool. At the top of the cylinder, six hydraulic pistons extract smoke in case of fire. From the entry, stairs and ramps lead to the dance floor below.

The rectangular plan has been inscribed by figures evocative of a cogwheel and gears: the contour of a great ellipse defines the outer bar

Alfredo Arribas and Miguel Morte 1991–93

Gran Velvet

Alfredo Arribas and Miguel Morte 1991–93

Gran Velvet

area and the inner dance floor is invaded by the two towers. The smaller cylinder contains lift access to a private club replicating the first Velvet bar. Toilets and cloakrooms add to the post-tech ambience and are located in double-height metal silos.

ADDRESS Poligono Montigalá, sector J C block IV, Badalona
CAR Rondas to Nus de la Trinitat, B-20 direction Montgat-Mataró, salida (exit) 3 Badalona Oeste-Montigalá
METRO L1 Fondo
ACCESS open Thursday, 24.00–5.00; Friday and Saturday, 18.00–22.00, 24.00–5.00; Sunday, 18.00–21.30

Alfredo Arribas and Miguel Morte 1991–93

Alfredo Arribas and Miguel Morte 1991–93

IKEA

Without any apparent planning, the area of Montigalá in Badalona has been built up with isolated stores with enormous surface area. Multinational firms have located themselves in this zone set tangentially to the city beltway system. These warehouse-type stores have become more prevalent and popular in the last few years, changing the habits of shoppers who flock to these exurban centres. They have also introduced a new typology to Barcelona, given the immense floor space required. The architects Antoni Poch and Jordi Moliner have built three interventions here, including a service station for BP, a store for Decathalon sporting goods and an IKEA store for the Nordic furniture company whose motto is 'It's a big country, someone's got to furnish it'. The architects have adapted the company's guidelines and the signature look used around the world to a difficult topography. The main difference is that parking is located underground instead of in an immense lot surrounding the building.

The building is composed of two colour-coded volumes. Set to the back and faced in blue corrugated metal is the immense windowless display and storage area with its one-way itinerary and exposed installations. In front with glazing and yellow corrugated-metal facing is a thinner volume housing the more social areas of the store: children's play area, information, pick-up services, lifts to car park and a bar and restaurant.

ADDRESS Carrer de Luxemburgo at the corner of Carrer de Grecia, Poligono Montigalá-Batlloria, Badalona
CAR Rondas to Nus de la Trinitat, B-20 direction Montgat-Mataró, salida (exit) 3 Badalona Oeste-Montgalá
METRO L1 Fondo
ACCESS Monday to Friday, 11.00–21.00; Saturday, 10.30–21.30

Antoni Poch and Jordi Moliner 1994–95

Antoni Poch and Jordi Moliner 1994–95

El Prat de Llobregat

Barcelona Airport Extension

Situated in the Llobregat river delta, an agricultural zone just outside the city, the original airport dates back to 1949. The terminal built in 1968 with a ceramic mural by Miró was enlarged during the Olympic period to service 12 million passengers per year. Plans are underway to redirect the river's course into the sea so that the industrial port may be enlarged and a third landing strip is proposed. The high-speed train from France to Madrid should stop here, making the airport into an internodal hub.

The 'Ramblas' of the airport addition co-ordinated by Peter Hodgkinson of the Taller is an 800-metre-long glazed shopping esplanade lined with freestanding glass kiosks containing duty-free shops, speciality boutiques, bars and restaurants. It forms the upper-level spine linking the new air-shuttle terminal, the remodelled terminal from 1968, and a new international terminal to one side with four triangular bays housing lounges and 24 telescopic finger footbridges for boarding. The Taller has combined grandiose abstracted classical concrete columns with a continuous aluminum-panel ceiling and red marble floor. The building is enclosed by a double glazed glass curtain wall hung off of a white metal structure, with a band of transparent glass at the level of the passenger. The interior is characterised by a sense of light, spaciousness and continuity. In the terminals all ticket offices and check-in zones are treated as smaller independent volumes within the container. International passengers enter into a sky-lit area marked by four palm trees.

ADDRESS El Prat de Llobregat
TRAINS RENFE to Aeroport from El Clot, Arc de Triomf, Plaça de Catalunya and Sants
AEROBÚS from Plaça Catalunya
ACCESS open

Ricardo Bofill – Taller de Arquitectura 1989–92

Ricardo Bofill – Taller de Arquitectura 1989–92

Igualada

Igualada Park and Cemetery

This is surely one of the most poetic works of Catalan architecture in recent years. The premature death of Enric Miralles at the age of 45, on 3 July 2000, was cause for a moment of reflection on his remarkable contribution. His youthful career was marked by invention, constant exploration and sensitive responses to the transformation of place. This competition-winning project was a collaboration with Carme Pinós. Conceived of as an earthwork, it forms a new landscape. The tectonic translation of the project from the delicate and beautiful drawings to built form revealed a hidden repository of ideas only hinted at by the fine tracings. In this site, enclosed by steep earth embankments, the topographical cues have been enhanced and moulded. The project incorporates and extends itself into its setting.

The site is located in an industrial area outside Igualada, a town in the interior of Catalunya, an hour's journey from Barcelona. The project was conceived as a processional path descending toward the burial area and the original design showed a zigzag gashed into the earth; this was later softened and curved. Scattered railroad ties set in the ground suggest a riverbed: they seem to be floating on the currents of a metaphorical tide of life. The path is lined by tapering concrete burial niches, with winged cornices. These repeatable pieces, skewed and fractured by the tensions of the earth behind, form retaining walls. Their curved upper forms act as overhanging parapets.

The procession ends in an elliptical court surrounded by gabions, walls of wire mesh containing stone that has been cut into the earth. Tombs covered by iron gates are dispersed on the various stepped terraces. Enric Miralles is buried here.

The funeral chapel, above to the left, is arrived at through a stair perforating the burial-niche wall. The triangular space is covered by a concrete

Enric Miralles and Carme Pinós 1985–91

Enric Miralles and Carme Pinós 1985–91

Igualada Park and Cemetery

roof slab with light streaming in through cut-outs above. The lateral sides are open.

The project celebrates rough, unrefined building techniques and textures. The concrete is rough, uneven, rugged, gravelly and textured. Materials have been used in unexpected ways. Reinforcement bars become sculptures, gates, and fences along the path of the geological promenade.

ADDRESS Avinguda de los Países Bajos, Igualada
CAR A7 direction Martorell, N2 to Igualada, salida (exit) 3, Poligon Industrial 'Les Comes' (Nou Cementari)
TRAIN FCG R6 to Igualada, leaving from Plaça Espanya six minutes after every hour. Taxi from station to the cemetery
ACCESS open

Enric Miralles and Carme Pinós 1985–91

Enric Miralles and Carme Pinós 1985–91

Index

Index

Index

Barcelona: a guide to recent architecture

PHOTOGRAPHS by Diego Ferrari except
pages 11.5 and 11.7 which are by Rafael
Vargas, reproduced by kind permission of
Alfredo Arribas Arquitectos Asociados.

México City

A guide to recent architecture

Visitors arriving in México for the first time are overwhelmed by the colour, richness, and the variety of Mexican life, a striking contrast to the USA. The twentieth-century architecture of México reflects this rich variety in a blend of local, exotic traditions and international avant-garde design and México City provides the best introduction to this architecture. Projects illustrated here include many building types, styles and development imperatives. Most are from the last ten years – a few earlier buildings of exceptional influence are included.

Inevitably, in a country where there are extremes of wealth and poverty, most of the buildings included are either for government institutions or for wealthy corporate or private clients. Some innovative work has been and is being done on low-cost housing both new buildings and renovations and improvements to existing areas and squatter settlements, work of overriding importance to the vast majority of the citizens of México City.

ISBN 1 84166 048 5
PRICE UK £10.00 US $15.00

Philip Opher with Xavier Sánchez Valladares

London

A guide to recent architecture

As ever, a version of the development of London's economic, political and cultural life can be read in the new buildings going up all over the capital.

After the excitement and farce of the city's millennium architecture (The London Eye, Peckham Library and Tate Modern on the one hand; the Dome and the infamous swaying Thames footbridge on the other), our rulers have built the lavish Portculis House for themselves; two new skyscrapers are nearing completion at Canary Wharf, now an astonishingly desirable address; industrial buildings are being renovated to house new-media firms and the people who own or work in them; and occasionally funding has been found for a school or public leisure facility. The city's decaying infrastructure has been boosted with the completion of the Jubilee Line extension.

This fifth edition of *London: a guide to recent architecture* brings the picture up to date.

ISBN 1 84166 060 4
PRICE UK £10.00 US $15.00

Samantha Hardingham